The Underground Guide to

Microsoft® Internet Assistant

About the Underground Guide Series

Welcome to the underground!

Are you tired of all the fluff—books that tell you what you already know, ones that assume you're an idiot and treat you accordingly, or dwell on the trivial while completely ignoring the tough parts?

Good. You're in the right place.

Series Editor Woody Leonhard and Addison-Wesley bring you the Underground Guides—serious books that tackle the tough questions head-on but still manage to keep a sense of humor (not to mention a sense of perspective!). Every page is chock-full of ideas you can put to use right away. We'll tell you what works and what doesn't—no bull, no pulled punches. We don't kowtow to the gods of the industry, we won't waste your time or your money, and we *will* treat you like the intelligent computer user we know you are.

Each Underground Guide is written by somebody who's been there—a working stiff who's suffered through the problems you're up against right now—and lived to tell about it. You're going to strike a rich vein of hard truth in these pages, and come away with a wealth of information you can put to use all day, every day.

So come along as we go spelunking where no book has gone before. Mind your head, and don't step in anything squishy. There will be lots of unexpected twists and turns . . . and maybe a laugh or two along the way.

The Underground Guide Series

Woody Leonhard, Series Editor

The Underground Guide to Word for Windows™:
Slightly Askew Advice from a WinWord Wizard

Woody Leonhard

The Underground Guide to Excel 5.0 for Windows™:
Slightly Askew Advice from Two Excel Wizards

Lee Hudspeth and Timothy-James Lee

The Underground Guide to UNIX®:
Slightly Askew Advice from a UNIX Guru

John Montgomery

The Underground Guide to Microsoft® Office, OLE, and VBA:
Slightly Askew Advice from Two Integration Wizards

Lee Hudspeth and Timothy-James Lee

The Underground Guide to Telecommuting:
Slightly Askew Advice on Leaving the Rat Race Behind

Woody Leonhard

The Underground Guide to Computer Security:
Slightly Askew Advice on Protecting Your PC and What's on It

Michael Alexander

The Underground Guide to Microsoft® Internet Assistant:
Slightly Askew Advice on Mastering the Web with WinWord

John Ross

The Underground Guide to

Microsoft® Internet Assistant

Slightly
Askew
Advice
on
Mastering
the
Web
with
WinWord

John Ross

Series Editor Woody Leonhard

ADDISON-WESLEY PUBLISHING COMPANY
Reading, Massachusetts • Menlo Park, California • New York • Don Mills, Ontario
Wokingham, England • Amsterdam • Bonn • Sydney • Singapore • Tokyo
Madrid • San Juan • Paris • Seoul • Milan • Mexico City • Taipei

Many of the designations used by manufacturers and sellers to distinguish their products are claimed as trademarks. Where those designations appear in this book, and Addison-Wesley was aware of a trademark claim, the designations have been printed in initial capital letters or all capital letters.

The author and publisher have taken care in preparation of this book, but make no expressed or implied warranty of any kind and assume no responsibility for errors or omissions. No liability is assumed for incidental or consequential damages in connection with or arising out of the use of the information or programs contained herein.

Library of Congress Cataloging-in-Publication Data

Ross, John
The underground guide to Microsoft Internet Assistant : slightly askew advice on mastering the Web with WinWord / John Ross.
p. cm. — (The Underground guide series)
Includes index.
ISBN 0-201-48944-9
1. Hypertext systems. 2. HTML (Document markup language).
3. Microsoft Internet Assistant. 4. World Wide Web (Information retrieval system). I. Title. II. Series.
QA76.76.H94R67 1996
025.04—dc20 95-45781
CIP

Sponsoring Editor: Kathleen Tibbetts
Project Manager: Sarah Weaver
Production Coordinator: Erin Sweeney
Cover design: Jean Seal
Text design: Kenneth L. Wilson, Wilson Graphics & Design
Set in 10 point Palatino by Rob Mauhar, CIP of Coronado

1 2 3 4 5 6 7 8 9 -MA- 0099989796
First printing, December 1995

Addison-Wesley books are available for bulk purchases by corporations, institutions, and other organizations. For more information please contact the Corporate, Government, and Special Sales Department at 800-238-9682.

Find us on the World-Wide Web at:
http://www.aw.com/devpress/

Contents

Foreword

Ready to hang your shingle out on the Web?

Worried that the Net life is passing you by?

Curious about World Wide Web pages, and what's really going on behind the scenes?

If you have that sneaky feeling that you probably could create a dynamite Web page—after all, every undergrad from here to Toledo seems to be able to master the process—you're probably right. And it won't cost $1,000 or $5,000 or whatever those fancy "Web consulting" companies charge these days. All you need is Word for Windows, a Net account, Microsoft's free Internet Assistant, and this book.

We aren't talking amateurish, "freshman" pages, either. Internet Assistant can produce world-class Web pages that are easily the equal of any pages you've ever seen. Drop by our Web site, http://www.wopr.com/wopr, for an eyeful.

In *The Underground Guide to Microsoft Internet Assistant*, Web expert John Ross will show you precisely how to set up an award-winning Web site using the extensive tools found in Microsoft's Internet Assistant. He covers everything from basic layout and design, through the creation phase, and on to more complex, more specialized topics like Forms and linking to CGI scripts.

Like the other Underground Guides, this book is packed with nitty-gritty advice that can come only from someone who has plunged into the depths of Internet Assistant—and lived to tell about it. The kind of advice you won't find anywhere else. It describes the easiest, fastest, best way to create a top-notch Web site, and leaves you with hundreds of ideas for tweaking the site to fit your needs.

Woody Leonhard
Series Hack
Coal Creek Canyon, Colorado

Acknowledgments

Thanks to Kathleen Tibbetts for her editorial guidance, and to Adam Tratt at Microsoft for technical assistance. Their attention has made this a better book than it would otherwise be.

Introduction

> You should make a point of trying every experience once, excepting incest and folk-dancing.
>
> Sir Arnold Bax
> Quoting 'A sympathetic Scot' in *Farewell, My Youth*, 1943

They're everywhere, it seems. The Internet in general and the World Wide Web in particular have become the citizens band radio of the mid-nineties. You can't open a magazine or newspaper without seeing yet another article or yet another advertisement with an address for somebody's Web page.

Everybody wants a Web page.

Twenty years from now, I suspect that having had your own personal Web page will be like having worn a Nehru jacket or a polyester leisure suit: something you're a little embarrassed to admit that you did. But right now it's a big deal. At the current rate, there will be more Web pages on the Internet than people in the world by about the year 2006.

So the bandwagon is rolling along, and you want to hop aboard. You want to tell the world about your hobby, your politics, or your business. Or you want to show everybody how cute your cat looks. It's time to add your own voice to the chorus of Webmasters.

If you know how to use Microsoft Word for Windows, you can use it to create Web pages without the need to learn yet another set of obscure commands. Internet Assistant, Microsoft's free add-on program, is all you need to convert word documents to HyperText Markup Language (HTML), the format that defines the way Web pages work. Assuming you've worked with Word's style sheet functions, you shouldn't have any trouble with HTML.

What do you want for free, features?

Well, maybe. Microsoft gives away Internet Assistant, so they've cut a few corners. That's an understatement; they've cut so many corners that Internet Assistant is just about spherical. The whole package is nothing but a program diskette (and you have to supply the diskette). At these prices, you don't get anything close to a manual, or even a simple instruction sheet. There are a few help screens, but that's about it. Before you can take full advantage of Internet Assistant's features and functions, you really need to understand how HTML works.

That's where this book comes in. *The Underground Guide to Microsoft Internet Assistant* will tell you how to obtain a copy of the program, how to install it on your PC, and how to use it with Word to create your Web pages. We'll also tell you about some of the HTML formats and functions that Internet Assistant has ignored, and explain how to add them to a document created with Internet Assistant.

And at no extra cost... a browser!

Internet Assistant is a pretty good HTML editor, especially for the price. But it also contains a built-in Web browser that you can use to import and view Web pages and other Internet files within Word. It's a browser, but not a very good one. If all the other browsers were as klunky as Internet Assistant, the Great Internet Boom of 1995 would never have happened.

It isn't as good as other free Web browsers, such as NCSA Mosaic and Microsoft's own Internet Explorer, but it's part of the package, so we've included a complete guide to Internet Assistant's built-in browser in this book. We'll also tell you how to use InternetWorks Lite, the hidden program that serves as Internet Assistant's Web browser engine.

Many people seem to be creating Web pages for the sake of creating Web pages. This is great for those of us who write books about creating Web pages, but you really ought to have a better reason than that to move forward. Like any other communications medium, the Web is close to ideal for some purposes and just terrible for others.

When you steal ideas from several sources, it's "research."

Before you start, please spend some time looking around the Internet at other people's Web pages. Not only can you swipe...uh, adapt some good design ideas and understand why bad ones don't work, but I hope you'll also think seriously about exactly what you want to accomplish. In many cases, some other publicity channel would be much more effective than a Web page, even though it won't be as fashionable. Remember that there are still about 240 million Americans and billions more around the world who don't have any way to see your Web pages. You can spend a lot of time and money messing with the Web without seeing any positive results.

Yes, it's true. I'm not convinced that the World Wide Web is going to replace print, television, cocktail parties, and shopping malls by the turn of the century. Useful? Yes. Interesting and entertaining? Absolutely. But a radical change in the way most people live their lives? I doubt it.

That said, I don't want to change your mind about making Web pages. In the right setting, they can be both effective and productive. You can use the information in this book, along with your existing knowledge of Word for Windows, to create Web sites that look just as good as the ones that people pay advertising agencies thousands of dollars to design. But remember that you didn't automatically start writing the Great American Novel (or the Great Canadian Novel, or the Great Sri Lankan Novel, or whatever) when you began using a word processor. There's no "Create a great design" command in Internet Assistant. Software is no substitute for design sense.

This book has four parts. Chapters 1 and 2 explain how and where to obtain the Internet Assistant software, and how to add it to your existing WinWord installation. In Chapters 3 and 4, you'll learn how to use Internet Assistant as a Web browser, and why you probably won't want to do so. You'll also learn how to bypass Word and work directly with InternetWorks. Chapters 5 through 10 are dedicated to planning, designing, and producing Web pages and other HTML documents. And finally, Chapter 11 is a preview of the new features in Version 2.0 of Internet Assistant, which works with Windows 95 and Word 7.0. After you've made it through the body of the book, you may want to refer to the Command Summary in the Appendix to find specific formatting tools.

Both Internet Assistant and this book share a common goal: we want to make your life a little easier. When you combine the two, you should be able to eliminate at least part of the drudgery of HTML editing. With any kind of luck, you might even enjoy yourself in the process.

1 Does the Internet Really *Need* an Assistant?

The perfect man has no method; or rather the best of methods, which is the method of no-method.

Shih-T'ao (17th century); quoted in Lin Yutang's
The Chinese Theory of Art

Internet Assistant is Microsoft's free add-on to Word for Windows that adds a HyperText Markup Language (HTML) template and an Internet browser to the base Word package. There are three possible reasons why you might be interested in using Internet Assistant. You might be an experienced Word for Windows user who wants to create World Wide Web pages or other HyperText Markup Language documents, or you want to add hyperlinks to online Word documents, or possibly you're looking for a cheap and dirty way to explore the Internet's World Wide Web. Internet Assistant lets you perform all of these tasks from within Word for Windows. InternetWorks Lite, an adequate but somewhat limited stand-alone Web browser, is buried inside Internet Assistant for Word 6.0. Chapter 4 shows you how to use InternetWorks without opening Word first.

Not wonderful, but free

Internet Assistant is not the best available HTML editor, nor is it the best Web browser you can find. It may not even be the best HTML template for WinWord. But it *is* free, which overcomes a multitude of limitations. If you're already a dedicated Word for Windows user, it may be easier to use Internet Assistant than to learn some other HTML editing program. And if you want to import material from the Internet into your own Word documents, building the browser into your word processor can be less painful than using the Windows Clipboard to move text or graphics from some other program.

It's not for everybody.

On the other hand, if you're one of the multitude who believe (with some justification) that all those formatting features and other bells, whistles, klaxons, and sirens in WinWord get in the way of text entry, Internet Assistant is not for you. If you're a devotee of some other word processor, or if you aren't particularly interested in creating your own Web pages or other hypertext documents, there's really not much point in buying and learning WinWord just to use Internet Assistant. There are easier and cheaper ways to get to the Internet, and less complicated ways to do HTML editing. And, of course, if you *really* want to understand HTML editing, you should become familiar with the codes that Internet Assistant automates and hides. (This is one of those "real programmers use assembly language" arguments, but it's still true.)

As a Web browser, Word for Windows is a fine word processing program. About the only time Word is likely to be your best choice for reading Web pages is when you plan to import text or graphics from a Web page into a Word document of your own. Otherwise, you're really better off using a dedicated Web browser such as Mosaic, Netscape, or Internet Explorer.

Since Internet Assistant is a freebie, you can play with it for a while without feeling that you've made a serious commitment to using it forever. After trying it, if you decide that Internet Assistant doesn't ring any of your personal chimes, you haven't invested a hundred dollars or more in a program you'll never use again.

This book is not a complete guide to using the Internet, nor is it a directory of the neat things you can find when you get there. It is a description of one particular Internet tool, Internet Assistant, which is available from Microsoft at little or no cost, and a guide to using that tool to navigate the World Wide Web and create your own pages on the Web. If you're a complete Internet novice, or if your previous exposure has been through a UNIX command line, this book will tell you what you need to know to set up a direct connection to the Internet. If you've already spent time using Mosaic, Netscape, or one of the other Windows-based Web browsers, you can use this book to learn how and where to put your own Web pages on line.

DO YOU REALLY NEED A WEB PAGE?

> 90% of everything is crud.
>
> Theodore Sturgeon

Why bother?

One question this book will *not* answer is why you would want to create Web pages in the first place. Having your own home page on the World Wide Web is this year's version of the lambada or the hula hoop; a lot of people are doing it because a lot of other people are doing it. At this stage in its development, much of the Web's effectiveness as a marketing tool remains to be proven.

If you're in the business of distributing information, the Web may be an efficient way to get that information to a lot of people at a relatively low cost; but a tremendous number of Web pages are either the online equivalent of junk mail, or ego strokes of the "this is me; this is my cat; here are some neat things that I've found on the Internet" variety. The novelty is likely to wear off after about three weeks.

To put this all in some kind of perspective, if the growth of the Internet business (not just the World Wide Web; the whole Internet, including hardware manufacturers, software developers, access providers, and people who write and publish books about it) meets current projections, it will reach about a billion dollars in 1998. That's about half of what Americans spend on hair dryers today. (I found those statistics on the Internet. That means they must be true, doesn't it?)

WHERE TO FIND INTERNET ASSISTANT

> If we don't find anything pleasant, at least we shall find something new.
>
> Voltaire
> *Candide,* 1759

Free, and worth every penny.

The first thing you need to know about Internet Assistant is how to lay your hands on a copy of the program. In most cases, the easiest way to obtain it is by downloading it from an online service, through the Internet, or from the Microsoft Download Service. If you prefer, you can order a copy on diskette, but you'll have to pay a few dollars for shipping.

Here are some places where you can find Internet Assistant:

- The Internet—If you already have access to a World Wide Web browser such as Netscape, or one of the Web browsers available through Prodigy, America Online, or some other online service, you can find Internet Assistant at Microsoft's Web site, http://www.microsoft.com. From the Microsoft home page, jump to the Microsoft Word page and look for the section about Internet Assistant. If you don't have a Web browser, there are a couple of other ways to get to Internet Assistant through the Internet. Using an FTP client, you can go to the archive at ftp.microsoft.com and look in the /softlib/MSLFILES directory. The Internet Assistant file for Word 6 is wordia.exe. The file for Word 95 is wordia2 (possibly followed by a release letter or number. If you have a Gopher client, go to gopher.microsoft.com, choose Access Software Libraries, and use the File name search tool to find wordia.
- CompuServe—Internet Assistant is available in the Microsoft Word forum (go msword) in the Word for Windows library. The easiest way to find it is to run a filename search for "Internet Assistant" or "wordia."
- America Online—To find Internet Assistant on AOL, use the Search Software Libraries command in the Go To menu. Search for the keywords "Internet Assistant" or "wordia."
- Microsoft Network—As you would expect, you can also download Internet Assistant from Microsoft's own online service. Look in the Computers & Software area, open the Software folder and then the Microsoft subfolder. You should find Internet Assistant in the Microsoft Office Family BBS under Microsoft Word. If you prefer, you can use the Find command in the Windows 95 Taskbar to search for wordia on the Microsoft Network.
- Prodigy—If you're a Prodigy subscriber, the best way to find Internet Assistant is to jump to Prodigy's World Wide Web browser and obtain the program from www.microsoft.com.
- Microsoft Download Service—If you don't have access to the Internet or an account with any of the online services, you can download Internet Assistant directly from Microsoft's own bulletin

board at 206-936-6735, or 905-568-3503 in Canada. The file you want for Word 6 is called wordia.exe. The Word 95 file is wordia2.exe (or some variation of wordia2.exe). Unless you live in metropolitan Seattle or near Cooksville, Ontario, you'll have to pay for the long-distance telephone call, which may be more expensive than connect time on CompuServe or America Online.

- Telephone Order—If you want your copy of Internet Assistant on a floppy disk with a genuine Microsoft label on it, it will cost you $5.50 for shipping and handling. To order, call Microsoft at 800-426-9400. Outside the United States, look in your Word manual for Microsoft Support Network telephone numbers, or call +1-206-936-8661. The part number for the WinWord 6 version of the Internet Assistant diskette is 059-151-655. Because Version 2 is still in beta test, Microsoft hasn't assigned a part number yet, but you can ask for it by name.

Wow! A Microsoft label!

WHAT YOU NEED TO USE INTERNET ASSISTANT

Necessity relieves us from the embarrassment of choice.

Luc de Clapiers Vauvenargues
Introduction to an Understanding of the Human Mind, Followed by Reflections and Maxims, 1746

Internet Assistant is not a stand-alone program; you must have a relatively recent English, French, or German version of Word for Windows to use Version 1; Version 2 also works in Italian. More specifically, you need Version 6.0a or later. If you're still using Version 2.0 of Word, you'll have to go off to your neighborhood software emporium or call your favorite mail-order place (why do they call it "mail order" when you order by telephone and they deliver by UPS or Federal Express?) and buy an upgrade. If you're using Windows 95, you should probably skip Word 6 and jump directly to Word 95. In that case, remember to use Version 2.0 of Internet Assistant.

Word 6.0a (at least)

If you already have WinWord 6 loaded on your computer, you must make sure the version is at least 6.0a. To figure out what you've got, start Word, drop down the Help menu, and select the About Microsoft Word command to open the window in Figure 1.1.

Figure 1.1 The Version number is in the first line of the About window.

Upgrading Word 6

Directly under the title bar, you'll find a line that says, "Microsoft Word Version 6.0" (or 6.0a or 6.0c or whatever). If it's 6.0 with no letter, you need the free patch that's available from the same sources as Internet Assistant. The filename for the U.S. version is word60a.exe. There are separate patch files for the Canadian, English, and Australian versions of Word.

Which language?

You should be able to figure out which language version you have by looking at it; if the menus and help screens are in French or German, you can be pretty certain that's the version. The differences between American, Canadian, Australian, and British English are a little more subtle. To identify the language version of Word you're using, you can create a simple macro:

1. Select the Macro command from the Tools menu.
2. When the Macro dialog box appears, type **Language** in the Macro Name field and click the Create button.
3. A new macro window will appear. Add these lines to the default text:

```
Sub MAIN
ver$ = AppInfo$(16)
MsgBox ver$ "Microsoft Word Language Version", 64
End Sub
```

4. Click on the Start button in the macro toolbar (the one with the solid arrowhead). An information window that identifies the language version like the one in Figure 1.2 will appear on your screen.

Figure 1.2 The Language macro displays the language version of Word.

The only language versions that will work with Internet Assistant are the various forms of English, French, and German (and Italian in Word 95). If you've got something else, you're out of luck for the moment. It's possible that future releases of Internet Assistant will work with other versions of Word, but Internet Assistant 1.0 is limited to those three languages.

There's one more thing you'll need to make full use of Internet Assistant: a connection to the Internet. You don't need to be on line to create HTML documents, but if you plan to use Internet Assistant (or InternetWorks) as a World Wide Web browser, you must have a TCP/IP connection to the Internet, and an interface program called a Winsock. We'll talk about Winsocks and Internet access in Chapter 3.

Chapter 2 explains how to install Internet Assistant and describes the changes that it makes to Word's toolbars and menus. In later chapters, you will learn about using the Word–Internet Assistant combination as a Web browser and an HTML editor.

2 Integrating Internet Assistant with WinWord

It is not enough to have a good mind. The main thing is to use it well.

René Descartes
Discourse on Method, 1637

One way or another, you've obtained a copy of Internet Assistant and confirmed that you have the correct version of Word for Windows to use it. Now what? It's time to install Internet Assistant.

wordia.exe

If you downloaded the program, you have a file called wordia.exe. This is a self-extracting file that has been compressed to reduce the amount of file transfer time needed. If you obtained the program on a diskette, you don't have to extract the Internet Assistant files. To extract the Internet Assistant files, copy the wordia.exe file to an empty temporary directory (c:\temp is always a good choice), and enter the command **wordia**. At this stage, it doesn't matter whether you're in DOS or Windows.

INSTALLING INTERNET ASSISTANT

In the beginning was the Word.

John 1:1 (King James Version)

Microsoft claims that it's possible to load Internet Assistant with 900 kilobytes of combined memory and free disk space, but in practice, it works a lot better with 3 megabytes or more. Before you try to install Internet Assistant, shut down any other programs that are currently active, including Word.

If your hard drive is down to its last 3 megabytes, you've probably got more serious problems than not being able to install Internet Assistant. Before you try to install *anything*, it's time to get rid of some of the useless files and programs that are probably cluttering up your drive, and transfer others to floppy disks. You should also give serious thought to installing a bigger hard drive or a disk compression program like Stacker or DriveSpace.

Actually installing Internet Assistant is simple: run "Setup." That's it. The Setup program runs you through a bunch of legal fine print and lets you choose a directory for the Internet Assistant files, but other than that, the whole process is automatic.

HOW INTERNET ASSISTANT CHANGES WINWORD

> Once a change of direction has begun, even though it's the wrong one, it still tends to clothe itself as thoroughly in the appurtenances of rightness as if it had been a natural all along.
>
> F. Scott Fitzgerald
> *The Crack-Up*, 1945

Internet Assistant automatically loads a global template into Word called wordhtml.wll, which adds some commands to the standard Word menus and a new button to the formatting toolbar. It also introduces two new command sets. When you start using Word to browse the World Wide Web and create new HTML documents, you will see completely new menus and toolbars.

Toolbars

The way toolbars should be organized in Word is one of those religious issues like the proper ingredients in a bowl of chili; it can start incredibly tedious arguments. Some people use the toolbars as they come out of the box without changing them; others hide them completely and use nothing but menu commands; still others add and delete buttons to personalize toolbars to meet their own needs and prejudices. *The Underground Guide to Word for Windows* (Woody Leonhard, Addison-Wesley, 1994) has an detailed explanation of how to modify toolbars and why you might want to do so. Everybody has an opinion about toolbars, and most of them are correct. The trouble starts when somebody else comes along and makes changes to your layout because "that's how it's supposed to be." People have committed murder with less justification.

That said, the samples in this book use the plain vanilla toolbars that Word provides at installation. If you've changed the formatting toolbar, it no longer looks like the ones you'll see in this book. Don't worry about the differences; right now, we're more concerned about the new buttons that Internet Assistant adds than the original layout.

Until you start browsing the Web or creating an HTML document, Word works exactly the same way that it did before you installed Internet Assistant. You can still create and edit documents, save them to disk, and print them to paper. There are a few new commands in the menus, but all the standard Word features are still there.

Most of the new features that Internet Assistant adds are in two alternative views: **Web Browse view** and **HTML Edit view**. As the name suggests, Web Browse view is Internet Assistant's World Wide Web browser. It has a completely different menu structure and toolbar from the normal Word layout. The changes in HTML Edit view aren't as extreme, but it also includes some new functions that aren't in the Normal template.

Text Editing

Just because you've loaded Internet Assistant, that doesn't mean you won't continue to use Word for other kinds of documents. Figure 2.1 shows the normal formatting toolbar after Internet Assistant has been loaded. Notice the button with the eyeglasses at the extreme left. When you click on this button, Word switches from the normal editor to Web Browse view, which is what you'll use to import Web pages and other Internet resources.

Figure 2.1 The button with the spectacles switches Word to Web Browse view.

Borderline problems

In order to make room for this new button, everything else on the toolbar has shifted one unit to the right; the original button at the right end is now gone. Losing the Borders button may or may not make an important difference to the way you work. If you don't do borders very often, it's no big deal; you can open the Borders toolbar from a menu command. If you use borders a lot, you've got several choices:

- Use either the Toolbars command in the View menu or the Borders and Shading command in the Format menu to display the Borders toolbar.
- Use the Borders and Shading command in the Format menu to add or remove borders.
- Use the Customize command in the Tools menu to add the Borders button to another toolbar.
- Use the Templates command in the File menu to unload the wordhtml.wll global template. You'll need to reload the template when you want to use Internet Assistant.

New Items in Menus

In addition to the new toolbar button, Internet Assistant also adds commands to several Word menus:

- To the File menu, Internet Assistant adds the Browse Web command.This command switches Word from a word processor to a Web browser. It has the same function as the Switch to Web Browse View button.

Browse Web = Web Browse

- To the View menu, Internet Assistant adds the Web Browse command. Oddly enough, Web Browse in the View menu is exactly the same as Browse Web in the File menu. (This is what happens when the programmer in charge of the File Menu doesn't talk to the programmer in charge of the View menu.)
- To the Insert menu, Internet Assistant adds the Insert HyperLink command. This command inserts a link in your document. A hyperlink may be a jump to another file or to another location in the same document. Hyperlinks are not limited to HTML documents; you can also add them to conventional Word files that are intended for online readers. Therefore, Internet Assistant makes the Insert HyperLink command available in the Text Edit view.

Web Browse View

Web Browse view is a completely new screen layout, with a quite different set of menu and toolbar commands, as shown in Figure 2.2. We'll talk about using these commands to move around the Internet in Chapter 3.

Figure 2.2 Web Browse view has a unique toolbar.

HTML Edit View

HTML Edit view is closer to Word's conventional text editing view, but it includes a handful of special commands that apply to HTML documents, such as the one that inserts a horizontal line, and a style sheet that recognizes the HTML tags. Figure 2.3 shows the HTML Edit View toolbar. You can learn about editing HTML documents starting in Chapter 5.

Figure 2.3 The HTML Edit View toolbar includes special commands for HTML.

REMOVING INTERNET ASSISTANT

Let me out!

If you decide that Internet Assistant is more trouble than it's worth, you can run the same Setup program you used to install Internet Assistant to permanently delete the files from your hard drive without messing up the rest of your Word installation. When Setup detects the existing installation, it will offer you the option of removing Internet Assistant.

It's also possible to temporarily remove Internet Assistant. To restore Word to its pre-Internet Assistant condition without deleting anything, follow these steps:

1. Open a new document.
2. Use the Templates command in the File menu to display the dialog box in Figure 2.4.

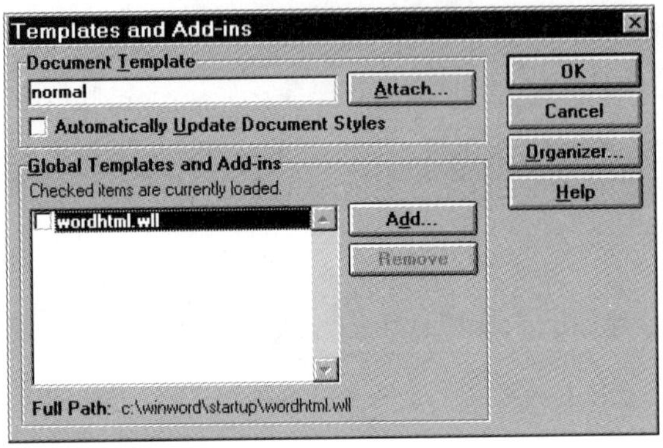

Figure 2.4 The wordhtml.wll add-in provides Internet Assistant functions.

3. Click on the box next to wordhtml.wll in the Global Templates and Add-ins list to remove the checkmark.
4. Click the OK button.

You can restore Internet Assistant later by loading the wordhtml.wll add-in.

3 Using Word as a World Wide Web Browser

'Tis true; there's magic in the web of it.

William Shakespeare
Othello

Before you try to create your own HTML documents or World Wide Web pages, you really should spend some time looking at some pages that are already up on the Internet. There are thousands of them, and more are appearing every day. Internet Assistant includes not just one, but two different Web browsers: one is integrated with WinWord, and the other is a separate stand-alone program.

Find a better browser.

The best advice I can give you about using Word as a Web browser is: Don't! Or if you must, use it once to download a free copy of NCSA Mosaic from http://www.ncsa.uiuc.edu, or Netscape Navigator from http://home.netscape.com. These programs (and several others that you can buy for under a hundred dollars) are much better browsers than Internet Assistant. For that matter, so is the hidden InternetWorks browser that we'll describe in Chapter 4. The Internet Assistant browser is subjectively slower than many others, it doesn't have as many features, and it doesn't know how to handle many common formatting commands. And since Netscape, Mosaic, and related browsers account for more than 80 percent of the total number of connections to most Web pages, you should use both of these programs to test any pages that you create because that's what most of your readers will be using.

But the Web browser is part of the Internet Assistant package, and it's easy to load it along with the HTML editor. Therefore, you will probably end up spending a little time playing with it, just to convince yourself that it's as mediocre as I've said it is. This chapter describes the Word browser's features and functions.

CONNECTING TO THE INTERNET: WINSOCK STACKS AND WHY YOU NEED ONE

Give us the tools and we will finish the job.

Winston Churchill, 1941

Before you can send a browser out onto the World Wide Web, you must have a TCP/IP connection to the Internet. **TCP/IP** is the set of commands and protocols that all computers on the Internet use to communicate with one another, and to control the routing and switching needed to find a path from one computer to another. More specifically, you need an interface file called a **Winsock** (Windows Sockets) stack that acts as the interface between application programs like the browser and the actual network driver.

What's a Winsock?

The Winsock standard is very much like the electrical sockets in your house. There's a standard interface (the plug and outlet) that works with many different kinds of appliances. You can use the same power outlet on your kitchen counter with a toaster, a blender, or a radio. A Winsock stack connects to a TCP/IP network (such as the Internet) rather than to Grand Coulee Dam, but it's also a standard interface that works with a variety of tools.

Universal interface

The Winsock standard is one of those all-too-rare cases in which the software industry actually cooperates across corporate lines. Any Winsock-compatible application program is supposed to work with any Winsock-compliant stack, and most of them actually work as promised. Therefore, you can mix and match applications from many suppliers and use them with whatever Winsock stack you happen to have on your computer. You can use the same Winsock stack with the Internet Assistant browser, with Netscape or Mosaic, and with dozens of other Internet applications.

On the other side of the interface, the Winsock stack exchanges data with a network driver (the stack and driver might be combined into a single program). If you use a modem and telephone line to connect your computer to the Internet, you need a driver that uses either SLIP (Serial Line Interface Protocol) or PPP (Point-to-Point Protocol). If you're on a LAN, you need the specific driver for your particular type of network. The advantage of this approach is that you don't have to change applications when you change your type of network access.

Figure 3.1 shows how a Winsock stack fits into the data flow between your system and the Internet.

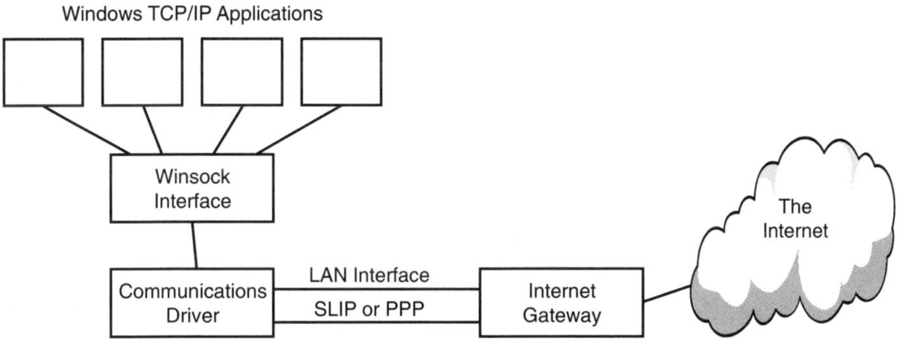

Figure 3.1 Data flow through a Winsock stack.

In practice, this means you can use Internet Assistant with any Winsock stack. If you can find a file on your hard drive called winsock.dll, you're in business. Your choices include:

- The Winsock stack included with Windows 95
- TCP/IP network connectivity products from WRQ, Distinct, TGV, FTP Software, and other suppliers
- Internet access products like Internet in a Box, Internet Chameleon, and IBM's Internet Connection
- Separate Winsock stacks available online from Trumpet Software and NetManage

Get help! Let George do it.

Configuring this stuff on your own can be painful, but you should be able to get somebody else to do much of the work for you. If you're on a LAN, your system administrator will probably want to install your Internet connection and Winsock stack. If you plan to use a telephone line and modem, you have a couple of choices: either buy one of the commercial products that automatically sets up an Internet account, or obtain a Winsock stack and a login script from your service provider.

The important thing to remember about a Winsock stack is that you only need to configure it once, unless you change service providers. If you already have TCP/IP access to the Internet, Internet Assistant and other application programs will automatically find and use your existing Winsock stack.

USING WORD AS A BROWSER

> A man travels the world in search of what he needs and returns home to find it.
>
> George Moore
> *The Brook Kerith,* 1916

Moving around the Web

The process of jumping around the World Wide Web with Internet Assistant will immediately be familiar to anybody who has used Netscape or Mosaic. Like those programs, it uses Uniform Resource Locators (URLs) to identify and locate Web pages and other files, hypertext links in contrasting colors, a list of bookmarks (which it calls Favorite Places), and other commands that are very similar to the ones in most other browsers. If you have used another browser before you start this one, you ought to be able to find your way around Internet Assistant without any hesitation.

When you start Word with the wordhtml.wll add-in, HTML Edit View mode is active. To use Word as a Web browser, you must switch to Web Browse view. There are three ways to do this:

1. Click on the button with the eyeglasses at the left side of the formatting toolbar.
2. Use the Browse Web command in the File menu.
3. Use the Web Browse command in the View menu.

The Word menu, the standard toolbar, and the formatting toolbar all change when you switch to Web Browse view. Figure 3.2 shows what they look like in Web Browse view.

Figure 3.2 The menu and toolbars change in Web Browse view.

Jumping to a Web page

In Web Browse view, Word can open and display World Wide Web pages in new document windows, just as it opens local document files. You can open a new Web page by clicking on a hypertext link or by using one of the commands in the menu or the formatting toolbar:

- Use the Open URL command in the File menu, or click on the URL button to jump to a specific location on the Web.
- Use the Open Favorite, History, Home, or arrow buttons in the formatting toolbar (or corresponding commands in the Tools and Window menus) to return to a page you've seen before.

As you know, Word does not close older documents when you open new ones. Unless you close them manually, old documents remain in their own windows within the Word screen. You can easily switch between documents with a few mouse clicks. When you're using Word as a Web browser, it opens each Web page as a new document. Therefore, you can return to any page you've seen during the current session by choosing that page from the list in the Window menu, or you can display more than one document at the same time by using the Arrange All command in the Window menu or the Maximize/Restore button in the upper right corner of each window.

The default maximum number of Web documents that can be open at one time is ten, which ought to be adequate for most purposes. To change the maximum, open the \windows\wordhtml.ini file and edit the AllowedOpenDocs= line in the [MISC] section.

In theory, Internet Assistant automatically finds your Winsock stack and connects your PC to the Internet when you request a jump to a Web page. However, it doesn't always work that way, especially if you're connecting to the Internet through a telephone line. If the automatic connection doesn't go through, you may have to start your Internet access program manually before you go into Web Browse view.

Creating a Useful Home Page

> You can have any kind of home you want. Why, you can even get stucco. Oh, how you can get stucco!
>
> Groucho Marx
> *The Cocoanuts* (screenplay by Morrie Ryskind), 1929

There's no place like home.

There are two different kinds of **home pages**. An information provider's home page is the top-level starting point for information about a specific topic with links to other related pages and files. As you move around the Internet, you will probably encounter many examples of this variety of home page. When we start to create HTML documents in Chapter 5, we'll use a home page dedicated to apple cider as a sample.

The other kind of home page is a default document that acts as home base within a Web browser. A home page generally has links to other frequently used locations such as Web directories. It may be located on the user's own machine or anywhere else on the Internet. Most browsers can be configured to automatically open the home page every time the user starts the program.

Internet Assistant doesn't display the home page automatically, but there's a button on the formatting toolbar that opens it, which is almost as good. You can also use the Home command in the Window menu to jump to the home page.

Faulty default

The default home page in Internet Assistant is a document called default.doc, which is shown in Figure 3.3. As it comes from Microsoft, default.doc is almost, but not quite, completely useless. It includes links to four other local documents, three of which contain information about using Internet Assistant. The fourth is the "Favorites" page, which you can open from the formatting toolbar without opening the home page. It would take at least two or three jumps from default.doc to get to any place you'd really want to go.

You have three options for creating a useful home page:

1. You can add more links to the existing default.doc.
2. You can create a new default.doc with links to your favorite sites.
3. You can replace default.doc with another document. Microsoft says the document may be "in any location," but in reality, that seems to mean any location on your own hard drive or local network.

Figure 3.3 The default Internet Assistant home page is not particularly useful.

The first two options don't accomplish very much. You can open a list of your favorite sites with the Open Favorite command in the formatting toolbar, so there's not much point to doing the same thing with the Home command.

A better approach is to download a copy of one of the online directories as your home page. These directories contain pointers to thousands of other Web pages, organized by subject. Here are a few directories to get you started:

- http://www.w3.org/DataSources/bySubject/Overview.html
- http://www.yahoo.com
- http://www.nosc.mil/planet_earth/everything.html
- http://wings.buffalo.edu/world/
- http://nearnet.gnn.com/gnn/wic/index.html

For example, here's how to change your home page to the Yahoo directory: **Yahoo!**

1. If it's not there already, switch Word to Web Browse view.
2. Connect your computer to the Internet.

3. Click on the URL button in the formatting toolbar and type **http://www.yahoo.com** in the Enter URL field. Click the OK button.
4. When the Yahoo home page in Figure 3.4 appears, open the File menu and choose the Save As command.

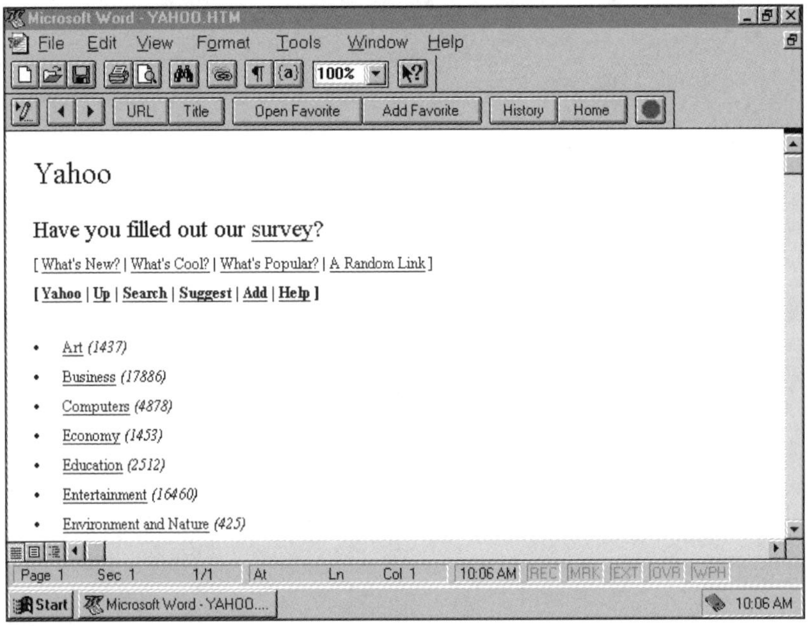

Figure 3.4 The Yahoo home page is a very good Web directory.

5. Change the filename to yahoo.htm and click the OK button.
6. Switch Word to Edit view.
7. Open the \windows\wordhtml.ini file.
8. Find the line in the [MISC] section that begins with "StartDoc=".
9. Replace the path currently in this line with the full path of the file you want to use as your home page. To use the Yahoo directory, change the line to:

   ```
   StartDoc=c:\winword\internet\yahoo.htm
   ```

   If you stored yahoo.htm in a different location, use the correct path for that location.
10. Choose the Save As command from the File menu.

11. Make sure the Save as Type field at the bottom of the Save As dialog box says "Text Only" and click the OK button to save the file.
12. Close Word. The next time you start Word, it will use the new document as your home page.

Word sometimes gives you an "Unable to load…" error message when you click on a link. If it happens once, try the same link again. If it happens on several different links during the same session, make sure your Internet connection is still in place. If you're still connected, close Word and restart it.

Moving Around the World Wide Web

Go on, Heathcliff. Run away. Bring me back the world.

Emily Brontë
Wuthering Heights, 1847

As a demonstration, let's spend some time exploring the Web. To begin, we'll use the Global Network Navigator (GNN) directory service to find pointers to other interesting sites.

1. If you're not already connected, connect your PC to the Internet now.
2. Switch Word to Web Browse view.
3. Click the URL button in the formatting toolbar.
4. When the Open URL dialog box appears, type **http://www.gnn.com/** in the Enter URL field. The GNN home page in Figure 3.5 appears on your screen.
5. Scroll down and click on "Best of the Net" under "Navigating the Net." Internet Assistant downloads the Web page shown in Figure 3.6. The "Best of the Net" list is a set of pointers to other Web pages that GNN's staff considers particularly interesting.
6. To view any of the sites on the list, click on the link to that site. For example, to jump to the New Zealand home page, scroll down to the list of "1994 GNN Best of the Net Honorees" and click on the link to New Zealand Information. When GNN's New Zealand Information page appears, click on "Go."

Let's go to Kiwi-land.

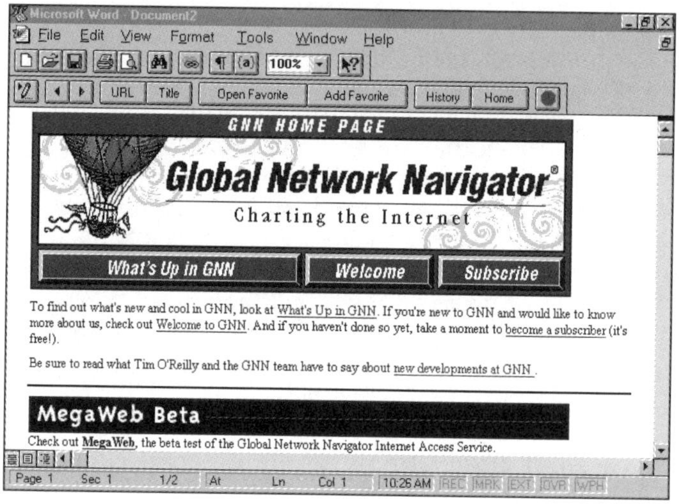

Figure 3.5 The Global Network Navigator home page.

Figure 3.6 GNN's Best of the Net Web page.

The New Zealand home page is yet another list of links, including news, tourist information, culture, and business data about New Zealand. To follow any of these threads, click on any underlined word or one of the graphics with a colored border.

You can access more than just Web pages with Internet Assistant. You can also reach Gopher servers and download text and data files from FTP archives. For example, follow these steps to use a Gopher server to download historical texts from the Queens Public Library in New York City:

1. Click the URL button in the formatting toolbar.
2. Type **gopher://vax.queens.lib.ny.us** in the Enter URL field and click the OK button.
3. When the menu in Figure 3.7 appears, select Social Sciences/History, and then Historical Documents.

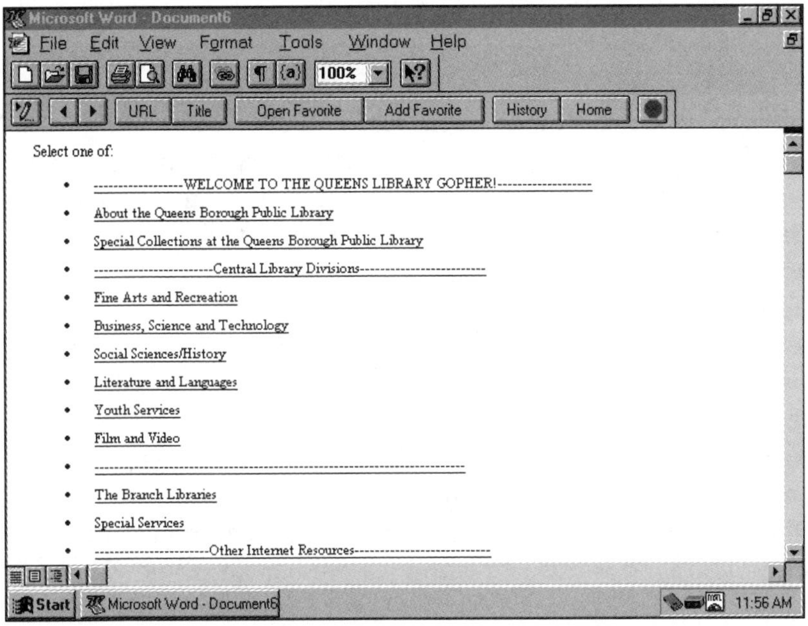

Figure 3.7 The top-level Gopher menu at the Queens Public Library.

4. Click on "Declaration of Independence" to transfer the text.
5. To save a copy of the text as a Word document, open Word's File menu and choose the Save As command. At the bottom of the Save As dialog box, drop down the File Type menu and scroll up to Word Document. Highlight Word Document, assign a new path and filename (such as july4.doc), and click the OK button.

IMPORTING TEXT FROM A WEB PAGE TO A WORD DOCUMENT

> I was set down from the carrier's cart at the age of three; and there with a sense of bewilderment and terror my life in the village began.
>
> Laurie Lee
> *Cider with Rosie,* 1959

In almost every case, your life will be much more pleasant if you use a separate Web browser instead of trying to navigate with Word and Internet Assistant. The one possible exception is when you want to copy text, graphics, or both from a Web page or other online resource and incorporate them into a document you're writing with Word. You could accomplish the same thing with a separate browser and the Windows Clipboard, but as long as you've already got Word open, you might think it would be a little more convenient to do it all within the same program.

However, Internet Assistant does not recognize all of the formatting instructions that other programs can handle without any difficulty. And when you switch to Edit view, you may get a bunch of irritating messages on your screen. Therefore, even this task, which would seem like a natural use for the Web browser within Word, may be easier through a separate browser.

How about herring jambalaya?

For example, Burk's Cafe is a Cajun restaurant located in a Norwegian neighborhood in Seattle. They don't serve blackened *lutefisk,* but they do have a presence on the Internet. Figure 3.8 shows one of their Web pages, imported to a PC using Netscape. Notice the background with little crawfish all over the page, the shaded border around the logo, and the fact that everything is centered.

Now look at the way Internet Assistant displays the same URL (in Figure 3.9). All you see is text, with everything pushed over to the left side. The entire graphic effect is lost. It's not as pretty, but all the text is there.

But it gets worse.

When you switch to Edit view, Internet Assistant shows you the location of every one of the formatting tags that it can't understand, as shown in Figure 3.10. If you copy this disaster to another Word document, you'll have to edit out all the <<Unknown HTML Tag>> messages before you can do anything useful with the text.

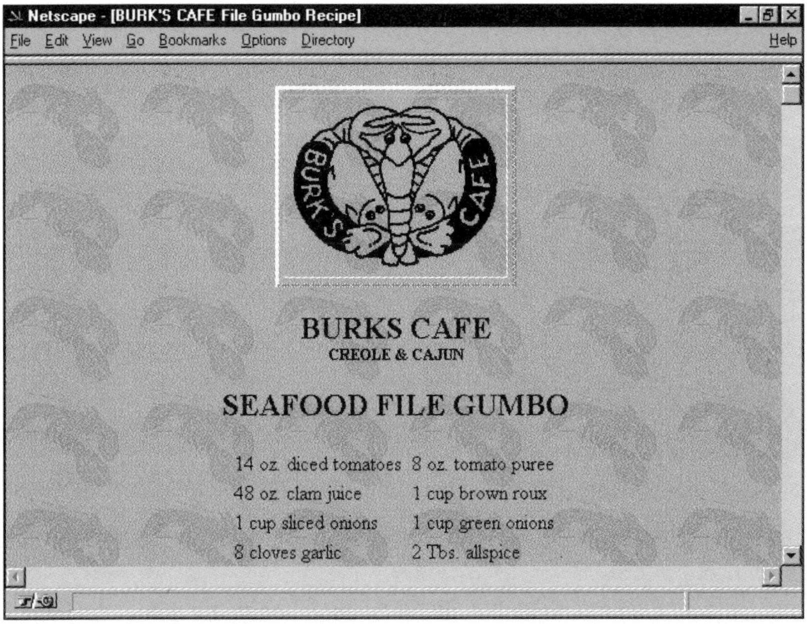

Figure 3.8 Burk's gumbo recipe, as Netscape sees it.

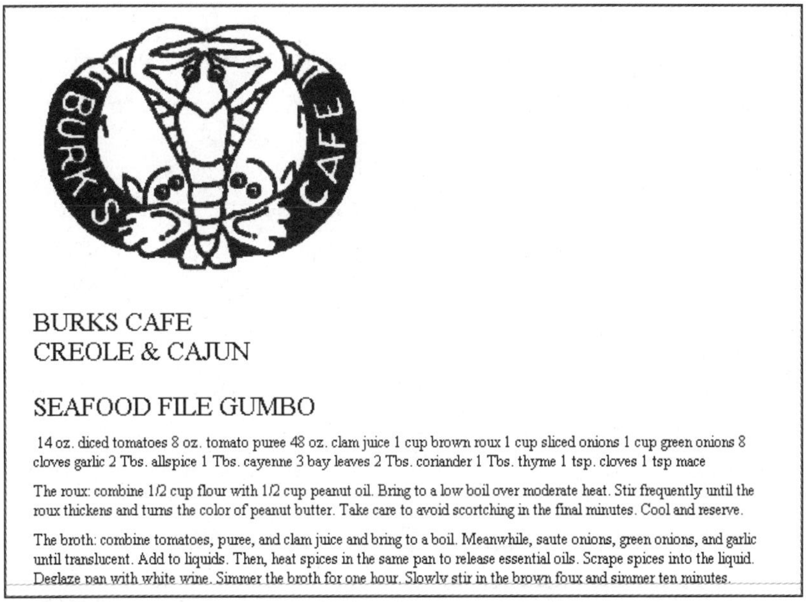

Figure 3.9 The same URL, using Internet Assistant.

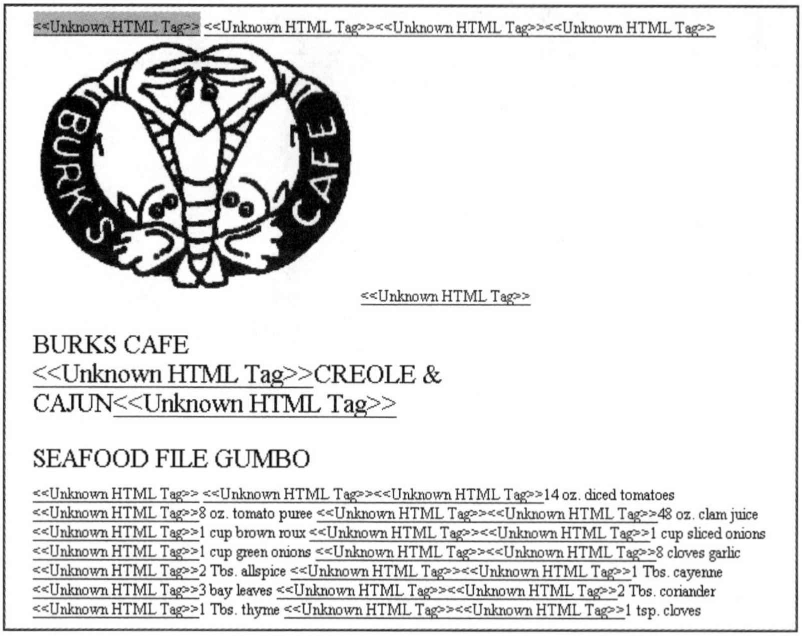

Figure 3.10 The Burk's recipe page, in Edit view.

It's not their fault.

To be fair, the reason for this problem is that many Web pages use tags that are not included in the industry-standard HyperText Markup Specification 2.0. After the specification was adopted, Netscape introduced a bunch of additional tags that other Web browsers were forced to either add or ignore. Strictly speaking, Internet Assistant is correct, and Web pages like the one from Burk's are wrong. But the fact remains that lots of noncompliant Web pages are out there, and Internet Assistant makes corned beef hash out of them.

This won't happen with every Web page, and it won't be a problem with text and graphic files that come from FTP or Gopher servers. But until you try to copy a Web page, there's no way to know if it contains unknown tags or not. And, unless you try to view the same pages with more than one browser, you won't know if you're seeing everything the designer intended.

You asked for it.

After all that, if you still want to use Word to import text to a document, here's the procedure:

1. Use Internet Assistant's Web browsing tools to find the document you want to copy. For example, the document in Figure 3.11 shows

the amount of information that can be contained in different kinds of storage devices. You can find the whole document at http://www.ccsf.caltech.edu/~roy/dataquan/.

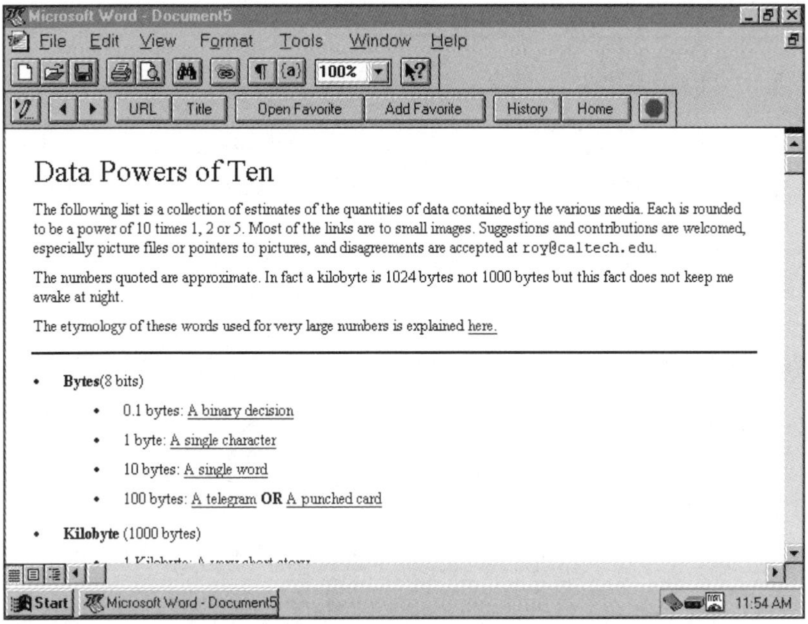

Figure 3.11 The Data Powers of Ten document.

2. To copy this document to a Word document, switch to Edit view. The icon button at the left side of the formatting toolbar changes from a pencil to a pair of eyeglasses.
3. If you're on a dial-in Internet connection, you can disconnect now.

At this point, this document is just like any other Word document, except that it may include one or more hypertext links. To edit it as a conventional text document, select the Save As command in the File menu, and choose Word Document as the file type. Word attaches the Normal.dot template to this document. To keep the hypertext links, save the document as HyperText Markup Language. To copy all or part of the text or a graphic element to another document, highlight the section you want to copy and use the Copy and Paste commands in the Edit menu.

Just because documents and illustrations are available on the Internet, it doesn't automatically mean that they are in the public domain. Many of the resources that you can find on line are protected by copyright. Therefore, you must obtain the copyright owner's permission before you duplicate or distribute them.

WEB BROWSE VIEW COMMAND SUMMARY

> Could I come near your beauty with my nails
> I'd set my ten commandments in your face.
>
> William Shakespeare
> *Henry VI,* Part 2, 1592

For the sake of completeness, here's a list of all of the Web Browse commands, with an explanation of each.

Standard Toolbar

Web Browse View adds two new buttons to the standard toolbar:

- Copy HyperLink

  The Copy HyperLink command places the URL of the current document in the Windows Clipboard. You can paste this URL into another Word document as a hypertext link. This command only works if the current document is a URL on the Internet. If the current document is located on your own computer, the link will not work.

- Show/Hide HTML

  Use the Show/Hide HTML command to see the HyperText Markup Language tags that are embedded in a document. If the tags are visible, clicking the same button will hide them.

Formatting Toolbar

The formatting toolbar in Web Browse view is completely new:

- Switch to Edit View

  Use the Switch to Edit View command to move from Web Browse view to Edit view.

-  Display Previous Screen

  Click the icon button with the arrowhead pointing to the left (backward) to return to the last Web page or other document.

-  Display Next Screen

  Click the icon button with the arrowhead pointing to the right (forward) to see the Web page or other document that you originally viewed immediately after the current screen. In other words, if you used the Previous Screen command to go back to an earlier screen, you can use the Next Screen command to move forward again.

- 

 Open URL

  Use the Open URL button to jump to a new Web page or other document. When the Open URL dialog box appears, type the Uniform Resource Locator that you want to see.

- 

 Title

  The Title button doesn't have anything to do with the Web Browser; you can use it to add a head element and other summary information to a new HTML document. (Head elements are explained in Chapter 6.)

- 

 Open Favorite

  The Open Favorite button loads the document that Internet Assistant uses as a hot list. A **hot list** is a place to note the URLs of Web sites that you expect to visit again in the future. Each item in the list is a hypertext link, so you can move to that site by clicking on its name. The default hot list is a document called favorite.doc.

- 

 Add Favorite

  Click the Add Favorite button to add the current document to your hot list. The next time you click on Open Favorite, the name of the new site will be at the bottom of the list.

  To remove a site from your hot list, open the hot list document and switch to Edit view. You can add or remove text from favorite.doc just as you would edit any other Word document.

- 

History

  Click the History button to display a list of the URLs that you have visited most recently. To return to a site on your history list, highlight the name of the site and click the Go To button.

  The default size of the History list is 50 items. You can change this number by editing the following line in the [Config] section of the windows\htmlhist.ini document:

  ```
  MRULength=n
  ```

  where *n* specifies the number of items in your history list.

  To remove an item from your history list, edit htmlhist.ini. There's an item in the [History] section and another in the [URL] section for each item in the list. To delete an item from the History list, you must remove *both* entries from htmlhist.ini.

- 

Home

  The Home command opens your home page, as specified in the wordhtml.ini file. (Home pages were discussed in detail earlier in this chapter.)

-  Stop

  Use the Stop button to interrupt Internet Assistant while it is in the process of downloading and formatting a Web page.

Menus

What's on the menu?

Internet Assistant also adds commands to the Word menus. Here are the commands that are related to navigating the World Wide Web:

File Menu

- Open URL command—jumps you to a new Web page or other Internet resource.
- HTML Document Info command—opens a dialog box where you can assign a title and other information to a local HTML document.

Edit Menu

- Copy HyperLink command—creates a jump to the current Web page in a document of your own. (We'll talk more about this command later.)

View Menu

- HTML Edit command—switches Word from Web Browse view to Edit view.
- Full Screen command—expands the current document to fill your entire display. If you're using Word to follow a series of links through the Internet, Full Screen display eliminates the distractions of toolbars, frames, and menus. To return to the conventional Word screen, click the small icon at the bottom of the screen, or press your Esc key.
- Load Images (on/off) command—downloads the text of a Web page being retrieved and then transfers each of the graphic images embedded in the page. Downloading large or complex graphics can take a long time, especially if you have a slow modem link. You could go out to the kitchen and make a sandwich while waiting for images to load, but in many cases, the images are more trouble than they're worth. When the Load Images option is on, Internet Assistant includes all graphic elements in Web pages. When Load Images is off, Internet Assistant transfers text, but ignores graphics.

Tools Menu

- Open Favorite Places command—loads your hot list.
- Add to Favorite Places command—adds the URL of the current document to your hot list.

Window Menu

- Go Back command—returns to the last Web page or other document.
- Go Forward command—moves to the next Web page or other document.
- Home command—opens your home page.

- History List command—displays a list of the last fifty URLs you have visited. To return to one of the places on the History list, highlight the name and click the Go To button.

In this chapter, you've learned everything you need to know about navigating the World Wide Web from within Word. In Chapter 4, we'll look at the Web browser that forms the hidden engine for Internet Assistant Version 1.0.

4 InternetWorks: The Hidden Web Browser Inside Internet Assistant

A man's most open actions have a secret side to them.

Joseph Conrad
Under Western Eyes, 1911

If you strip out all the Microsoft Word trappings from Internet Assistant 1.0, you're left with a somewhat underpowered version of Booklink's InternetWorks Web browser. Depending on which dialog box or information window you open, the program is called either **InternetWorks Lite** or **InternetWorks Internet Assistant**. Either way, it bears about the same relationship to a head-of-the-pack browser like Netscape (or even the full-featured version of InternetWorks) as a light American lager beer has to a Bavarian Pilsner—it's missing a lot of the flavor.

Your basic, no-frills browser

To be more specific, this version of InternetWorks does not have a hot list, it does not support mail or news, and nothing happens when you look for online help. The lack of a hot list is reason enough to use some other program when you want to do any serious Web browsing.

Multiple Windows

InternetWorks does have one nice feature that isn't in many other browsers: you can split the document window into two or more smaller panes and then move around the Internet separately in each pane. Therefore, you can use one pane to download a large or complex Web page or other document while you are reading a document in another pane.

Booklink is owned by America Online, and they use roughly the same screen layout and internal software engine in their own Web browser products. If you're an America Online subscriber, or if you have used their separate GNNWorks product, you will recognize InternetWorks for Internet Assistant.

Unless you want to import Web pages into Word documents, InternetWorks is a better way to navigate the Internet than using Web Browse mode within Word, but that's sort of like saying that a garden shovel is better than a teaspoon for clearing snow off your driveway—you really need a full-size snow shovel. For serious Internet navigation, you should use something like Netscape, Mosaic, or the shrink-wrapped version of InternetWorks. Apparently, Microsoft agrees with this judgment, because they've replaced InternetWorks in the Word 95 version of Internet Assistant. This is no great loss. If you're using Windows 95 and you don't already have a Web browser, take a look at Internet Explorer from Microsoft or Netscape Navigator from Netscape. They're both much better browsers than the one in Internet Assistant.

As long as it's there...

You get InternetWorks Lite when you load Internet Assistant, whether you need it or not (unless you instruct Internet Assistant Setup to completely bypass Internet browsing components), and Internet Assistant's Web Browse mode won't work without InternetWorks, so you can't just delete it. You might as well know something about using it.

STARTING INTERNETWORKS

> No degree of dullness can safeguard a work against the determination of critics to find it fascinating.
>
> Harold Rosenberg
> *Discovering the Present*, 1973

When you install Internet Assistant, the Setup routine creates a subdirectory under the WinWord directory called \Internet. It also loads some files into other directories, but we don't need to worry about them right now. When you run Internet Assistant within Word, it automatically loads the Internet files as it requires them.

One of these files is iwia.exe, the Web browser program. To start InternetWorks without messing with Word, run this program file from Windows. If you plan to use it more than once or twice, you will want to put it in a program group (in Windows 3.X) or create a shortcut in the Windows 95 desktop or Programs menu.

THE INTERNETWORKS SCREEN

> Everything is worthy of notice, for everything can be interpreted.
>
> Hermann Hesse
> *The Glass Bead Game,* 1943

Unless you have changed your home page, you'll see the screen shown in Figure 4.1 when you start the Web browser program. Let's take a quick tour.

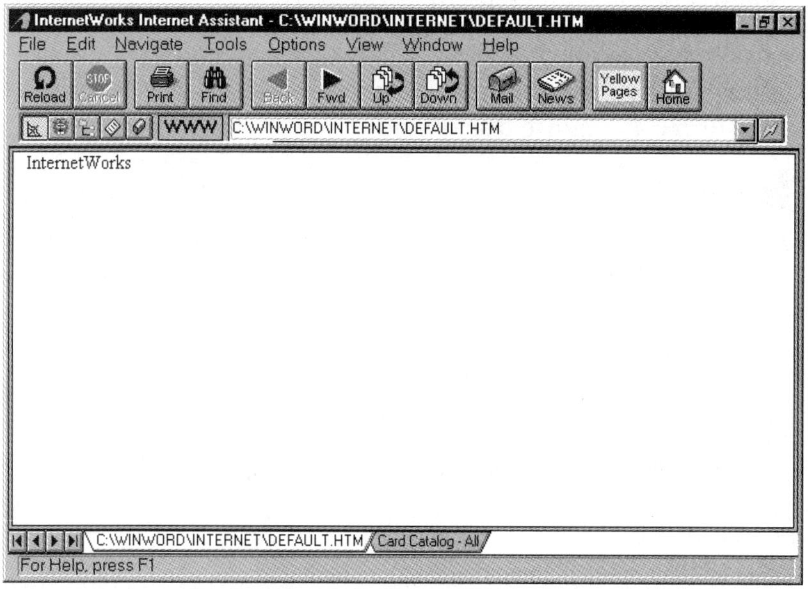

Figure 4.1 The main InternetWorks screen.

The InternetWorks Toolbar

The do-nothing buttons

The InternetWorks toolbar claims to contain a dozen buttons for "commonly used commands," but three of them don't do anything: the Mail, News, and Yellow Pages buttons are all left over from some other version of InternetWorks that does not exist any more—if you call the toll-free number that appears when you click one of these buttons, a nice man will explain that America Online would like you to subscribe to their Internet service and he'd be just delighted to take your credit card number (well, it was a man when I called, and he kept calling it "American Online").

These are the other toolbar buttons:

- 

Reload

  The Reload command instructs InternetWorks to start loading the current document again from the beginning. There are at least two occasions when you should use this command:

  1. When you're connected to a Web page that updates itself frequently.
  2. When you're in the middle of a download that stops before it has transferred the entire document.

- 

Cancel

  The Cancel command interrupts a document download before it is complete. Use this command if you change your mind and decide that you don't want to download a document after you have requested it.

- 

Print

  The Print command sends the current document to your printer.

- 

Find

  The Find command searches for a string of text within the current document.

- 

Back

  The Back command moves you to the Web page or other document from which you opened the current screen.

- 

Fwd

  The Forward command returns you to the link to which you most recently moved from the current page.

- 

Up and Down

  The Up and Down commands treat open Web pages and other documents in each pane as if they are a stack of papers; use the Up and Down commands to move up and down the stack. InternetWorks treats each stack as a closed loop—when you reach the bottom, the next page will be the top of the same stack.

- 

Mail, News, and Yellow Pages

  These three commands don't do anything useful. If you try to use one, you get an un-helpful information window.

- 

Home

  Click on the Home command button to return to your home page. InternetWorks has a completely worthless default home page. In order to use something else as your home page, you must replace the existing \winword\internet\default.htm file with a new default.htm file with some useful links. You have two choices: you can use Internet Assistant or any other HTML editor to create your own home page, or you can save a copy of an online directory such as http://www.yahoo.com or one of the others listed in Chapter 3. Either way, you must save the file as default.htm in your \winword\internet directory. (Windows 95 calls directories "folders," but we all know that they're really still directories. If it has webbed feet and quacks....)

Protocol Accelerator Buttons

A matter of protocol

InternetWorks calls the smaller buttons under the main toolbar **Protocol Accelerator buttons**, which is an awfully fancy name for something that does nothing except replace a handful of keystrokes. (See Figure 4.2.) Each button corresponds to a type of Internet service—World Wide Web, Gopher, FTP, News, and Mail—and when you click that button, the correct heading for that URL appears in the URL Combo Box, to the right of the buttons.

Figure 4.2 InternetWorks Protocol Accelerator buttons.

URL Combo Box

The **URL combo box** is the field where you specify the URL of a Web page, Gopher server, FTP site, or other Internet resource that you want to display in InternetWorks. (See Figure 4.3.) It's a "combo box" because it doubles as a history display; use the arrow button at the right side of the box to drop down a menu that lists the URLs of all the documents you have seen during the current browsing session. Click on a listing in the history menu to move it to the current URL field. To download the URL listed in the combo box, click the button with the lightning bolt.

Figure 4.3 InternetWorks URL combo box.

Tab List

The **tab list** under the document window contains a tab for every Web page or other document you have seen during the current session. (See Figure 4.4.) Click on a tab to return to that page. The arrow buttons at the left side of the tab list scroll the tabs to the left or right, one tab at a time and one page at a time.

Figure 4.4 InternetWorks tab list.

MOVING AROUND THE INTERNET WITH INTERNETWORKS

> The poetry of motion! The *real* way to travel! The *only* way to travel! Here today—in next week tomorrow! Villages skipped, towns and cities jumped—always somebody else's horizon! O bliss! O poop-poop! O my! O my!
>
> Kenneth Grahame
> *The Wind in the Willows*, 1908

InternetWorks provides quite a few methods for opening Web pages and other documents:

- Links appear in documents in a contrasting color. When you move your cursor to a link, the link's URL appears in the status bar at the bottom of your screen. Click on a link to jump to the URL.
- Type a URL in the URL combo box and click the lightning bolt button.
- Drop down the history list in the URL combo box and click on the document you want.
- Use the Open Local File or Open URL command in the File menu to open a dialog box or browser where you can specify the document you want.
- Click on a tab in the tab list at the bottom of the document window to return to that page.
- Click on the Back or Fwd button in the toolbar to retrace your steps through links you've already seen during the current session.
- Click on the Up or Down button to return to documents you've displayed in the current session. The difference between Up/Down and Fwd/Back is that Up and Down include every page you've seen, whereas Forward and Back retrace links, so you don't revisit every blind alley.
- Click on a Card Catalog tab in the tab list or use one of the Card Catalogs commands in the Tools menu to open a catalog of documents you've opened during the current session like the one in Figure 4.5. To return to the URL listed on a "catalog card," click the arrow button at the right side of the listing.
- Click the Home button in the toolbar to return to default.htm.

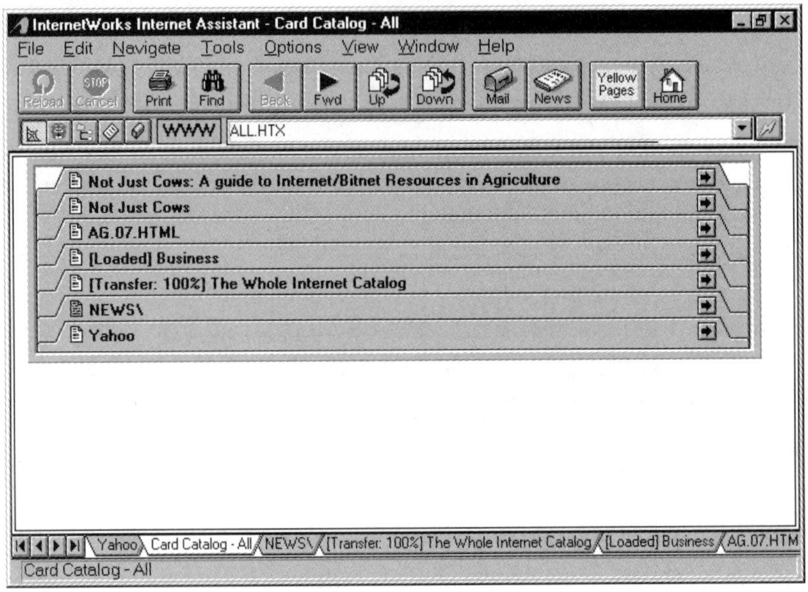

Figure 4.5 An InternetWorks card catalog.

SPLITTING THE DOCUMENT WINDOW

> The art of war is to dispose one's troops so that they are everywhere at the same time.
>
> Napoleon, 1806

Window panes When you're following a series of links through the World Wide Web, or if you're downloading a large file, you may want to split the document window into two or more panes, and follow separate threads in each pane.

When the document window has more than one pane, only one pane is active. The toolbar buttons and menu commands control the active pane. You can make any pane active by clicking your mouse within that pane. If you prefer, you can move to the next pane by pressing Ctrl+F6.

It will be a lot easier to figure out which pane is active if you set the Active Border Color to a contrasting color. In Windows 3.X, you can change colors from the Control Panel in the Main program group. In

Windows 95, right-click anywhere on your desktop, select the Properties command, and choose the Appearance tab.

To open a new pane within the document window, open the Window menu and use either the Split Horizontally or Split Vertically command. Initially the new pane has the same contents as the active pane, but when you follow a thread or use one of the other tools to move to a new Web page or other document, only the active pane changes. Figure 4.6 shows InternetWorks with four different Web pages visible. The active pane is the one in the upper left, with the dark border.

Figure 4.6 Multiple Web pages in a single view.

Eight is enough.

You can open as many new panes as you want, but after you get to about eight separate panes, each one is really too small to be much use. To change the size of a pane, drag the border you want to move.

RIGHT MOUSE MENUS

House-keeping ain't no joke.

Louisa May Alcott
Little Women, 1868–69

The mouse is always right.

Like many other Windows programs, InternetWorks displays a popup menu when you click your right mouse button. The commands in these menus depend on the location of the cursor and the activity that is taking place at the time. For example, if you right-click while you are transferring a file, the menu includes a Cancel Transfer command.

Most of the right-click commands are duplicates of commands from the menu and the toolbar, but the following commands are only available in a right-click menu:

- **Copy URL to Clipboard**—This command appears when you right-click inside a document window. If the cursor is over a link, the Copy URL to Clipboard command places the URL of that link on the Windows Clipboard. If the cursor is anywhere else within the document window, the command places the URL of the current Web page or other document on the Clipboard.
- **Link to URL**—This command appears when you right-click a link or a card in the card catalog. When the cursor is over a link, the Link to URL command opens the URL dialog box, with the URL of the selected link in the Uniform Resource Locator field. From a catalog card, it takes you to the URL listed on the card.
- **Save Image**—This command appears when your cursor is over an image in a Web page. Use the Save Image command to store a copy of the current image file on your hard drive.
- **Sort Catalog**—This command appears when you right-click from the card catalog. It opens a submenu of options for the order in which the card catalog displays cards.
- **Remove Card**—The Remove Card command deletes the current card from the card catalog.
- **More Info**—The More Info command appears when you right-click from the card catalog. It displays an information window which provides more details about the current card. This is the

same information you get when you use the Document Info command in the Window menu.

INTERNETWORKS COMMAND SUMMARY

> The capacity of human beings to bore one another seems to be vastly greater than that of any other animals.
>
> H.L. Mencken, 1956

InternetWorks for Internet Assistant includes these commands.

File Menu

- **Open Local File**—Use the Open Local File command to display a HyperText Markup Language (HTML) file or a document located on your own system or on a network drive in the InternetWorks document window.
- **Open URL**—Use the Open URL command to download a Web page or other Internet resource to InternetWorks.
- **Close**—Use the Close command to close the document in the active pane of the document window.
- **Save As**—Use the Save As command to store a copy of the active Web page or other document on your hard drive.
- **Reload**—Use the Reload command to download a new copy of the currently active Web page or other document.
- **Play**—Use the Play command to play an audio file. This command only works when there's an audio file attached to the current Web page or other document and you have used the Viewers command in the Options menu to associate an audio player program with the audio file's file extension.
- **Print**—Use the Print command to print a copy of the active Web page or other document.
- **Print Preview**—Use the Print Preview command to display a reduced full-page view of the current Web page or other document, as shown in Figure 4.7. This image is identical to the layout of a

printed copy of this page. Use the Zoom In and Zoom Out buttons or double-click on the image to change the size of the image.

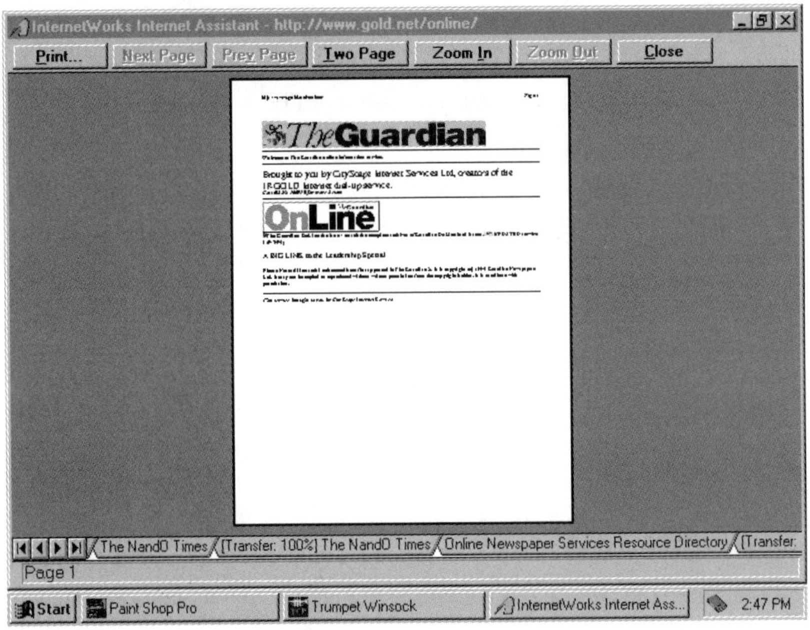

Figure 4.7 The Print Preview window.

- **Print Setup**—Use the Print Setup command to change printers, page size, and other properties, and to switch between portrait and landscape orientation.
- **Page Layout**—Use the Page Layout command to open the dialog box in Figure 4.8, which controls the number of columns and the size of the margins on the printed page.
- **History Listings**—InternetWorks displays the four most recent URLs in the File menu. Select one of the history listings to return to the URL named in that listing.
- **Send Mail**—The Send Mail command does not work in this version of InternetWorks.

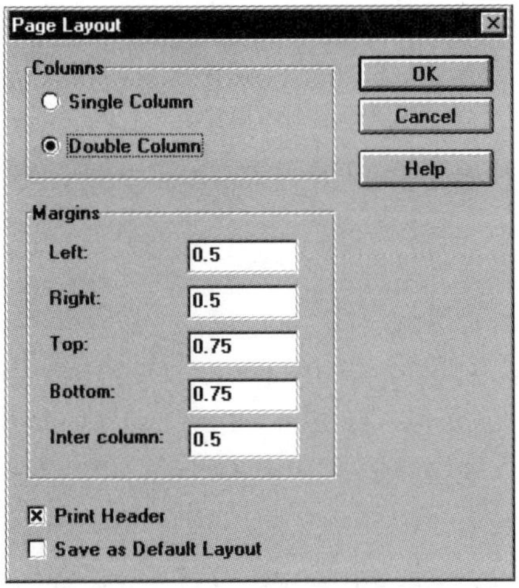

Figure 4.8 The Page Layout dialog box.

Edit Menu

- **Undo**—Use the Undo command to cancel your most recent action.
- **Cut, Copy, Paste,** and **Paste Link**—These commands do nothing in this version of InternetWorks.
- **Find**—Use the Find command to search for a word or other character string in the current Web page or other document.

Navigate Menu

- **Back**—Use the Back command to return to the URL from which you jumped to the current Web page or other document.
- **Forward**—Use the Forward command after you use the Back command to return to the next URL.
- **Up and Down**—When you open a new Web page or other document, InternetWorks holds the old page under the new one. Use the Up and Down commands to move through the stack of pages in the active pane of the document window.

Tools Menu

- **Mail and News**—The Mail and News commands do not work in this version of InternetWorks.

- **Card Catalogs**—The Card Catalogs command opens a submenu with a list of URL types. Select a command from the submenu to create a new card catalog that includes all of the currently open URLs of the specified type, including URLs that are not currently visible.

Options Menu

- **Load Images**—Use the Load Images to instruct InternetWorks to include or ignore graphic images when you download Web pages. If you do not load images, it will take a lot less time to transfer documents.
- **Layout**—Use the Layout command to change the on-screen display of Web pages and other documents.
- **Fonts**—Use the Fonts command to specify the typefaces that InternetWorks uses to display and print text marked with HTML tags in Web pages.
- **User**—The User command opens a dialog box where you can fill in your name and e-mail address. However, because this version of InternetWorks does not use this information for anything, it really doesn't make any difference what you put in these fields.
- **Viewers**—Viewers are utilities and application programs that InternetWorks uses to open and display files that it downloads. To associate a file extension with an application, use the External Viewer Configuration dialog box in Figure 4.9 to assign a viewer program for each file type that you expect to download.

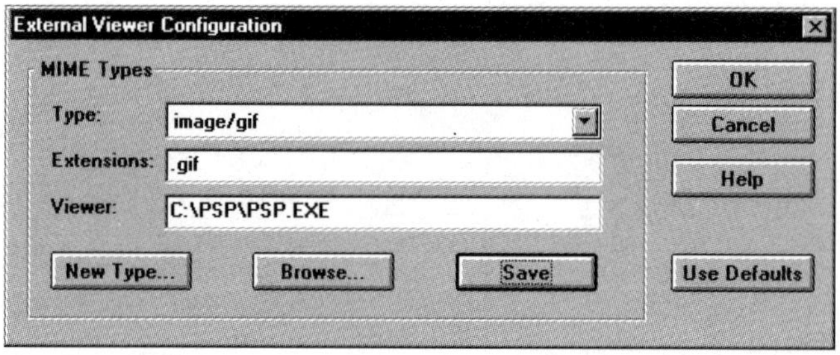

Figure 4.9 The External Viewer Configuration dialog box.

If you associate graphic file extensions with an external viewer, both InternetWorks and Internet Assistant will open the external program every time they encounter a .gif or .jpg file embedded in a Web page, rather than placing the image in the Web page. If a single page has several images, a separate copy of the viewer program will open up for each image. You don't want this to happen. Really you don't. Therefore, you should not assign graphic images to an external viewer.

- **Proxy Servers**—The only time you need to worry about proxy servers is when you're connecting to the Internet through a secure LAN with firewalls to keep unauthorized eyes out of your network's files. If you're on a secure LAN, obtain IP addresses and port numbers for each type of proxy server from your system administrator or help desk and type them in the Proxy Servers dialog box.

View Menu

- **Toolbar**—Use the Toolbar command to display or hide the InternetWorks toolbar.
- **Status Bar**—Use the Status Bar command to display or hide the status bar at the bottom of the screen.
- **Scraps**—Use the Scraps command to display or hide the tab list. No, I don't know why they're called "scraps."

Window Menu

- **Split Horizontally** and **Split Vertically**—Use either of the Split commands to divide the currently active pane into two smaller panes. Each new pane will contain the same URL, but you can follow different links in each one.
- **Close Pane**—Use the Close Pane command to close the active pane.
- **Document Info**—Use the Document Info command to open an information window with details about the currently active URL.
- **Cancel Download**—Use the Cancel Download command to interrupt a file transfer before it is complete.

If you've read through this entire chapter, you are probably a good candidate for the full version of InternetWorks, which is a far better browser than this crippled version would suggest. If you really like InternetWorks, take a look at Booklink's home page at http://www.booklink.com. It's possible that they might still have a beta or release version available there for free download. You can also find information on the latest and greatest enhancement of InternetWorks from http://www.megaweb.com, or on America Online (keyword Megaweb).

5 Planning an HTML Document

It may be that the whims of chance are really the importunities of design. But if there is a Design, it aims to look natural and fortuitous; that is how it gets us into its web.

Mary McCarthy
On the Contrary, 1962

Now that you've had a chance to explore the World Wide Web on your own, you're ready to start thinking about creating your own HTML documents. No, that's not right. You've *been* thinking about it, or you wouldn't be reading this book. It's time to start planning a document.

Plan before you write.

It might be more fun to jump right in and start coding, but you're less likely to get into trouble if you create a blueprint before you begin to spin your own section of the World Wide Web. This chapter explains how to plan a Web site. Even if you only plan to create a single page rather than an interconnected set of pages, the information in this chapter may help you understand the structure of your project.

Internet Assistant lends itself to two quite different kinds of documents: self-contained hypertext documents that you distribute on disk or through a LAN, and World Wide Web pages, which you place on a server connected to the Internet or a smaller private network. In a self-contained document, all of the links are to other parts of the same document or to other documents on the same disk. For example, you might create a User's Manual for a complicated piece of hardware or software with "live" cross-references to a glossary, a command summary, and more detailed descriptions of individual components. (We'll create a self-contained hypertext document in Chapter 6.)

DEFINING YOUR TOPIC

> A man may fulfil the object of his existence by asking a question he cannot answer, and attempting a task he cannot achieve.
>
> Oliver Wendell Holmes, Sr.
> Cited in *Life and Letters of O.W. Holmes,* by John Morse

Links in Web pages may be to other documents or files located anywhere on the Internet. A Web page might have pointers to other pages on the same server, to related pages on other servers, or to some of each. In many cases, you're really talking about creating a set of interconnected Web pages rather than a single page. This set of pages is sometimes called a **Web site**.

What kind of Web site?

Before you do anything else, take some time to understand exactly what you want to accomplish with your Web site. Are you trying to promote a business or share information about your hobby? Do you want people who visit to order a product, or write a letter to a senator, or plant a tree? Or is the page simply intended to amuse, outrage, or inform a reader? There are hundreds of thousands of Web pages out there; why should anybody want to visit yours?

The purpose of your site may dictate the form. If you are using the Web to publish a catalog or to provide pointers to other Internet resources, a hub-and-spokes design might be the best approach. On the other hand, a Web site that presents a narrative should probably be more linear.

CREATING AN OUTLINE

> If you wish to advance to the infinite, explore the finite in all directions.
>
> Johann Goethe
> *Miscellaneous Epigrams*

It's essential to know where you want to lead your readers before you start. After you decide what your Web site should accomplish, the next step is to figure out what information you need to provide to meet that goal. Specific elements of your Web site plan may change after you start creating individual pages, but if you don't use some kind of a road map as a guide, you may never know that you have changed course in mid-project, or that you've led your visitors to one or more unintended dead ends. Your **outline** should be the bridge between the original idea and the final product.

Start with an outline.

As an example, let's consider a Web site dedicated to growing and using tree fruit. In the Tree Fruit Home Page, you'll include brief descriptions of the information in each additional page in the site and links to other sites that contain information about apples, peaches, pears, and plums.

Hypertext doesn't have to be linear because you can jump around among related subjects and follow multiple threads from a single starting point. However, while you're planning your Web site, it's important to give yourself an idea of just exactly what you want to accomplish and what information you want to include. There are at least two ways to get started:

1. Create a more-or-less traditional outline.
2. Draw a free-form "mind map."

If you tend to think in organized steps, a linear outline is the better choice; if you can juggle many mental objects at the same time, you might want to try using a mind map.

Remember sophomore English? Why?

You remember outlines from high school. Like many other things you learned in high school—algebra, your locker combination, and how to get excused from gym class—you probably haven't messed with the formal rules of outlining since you graduated. Neither have I. Your Web site outline doesn't have to be formal, just as long as it makes sense to you. Nobody will reduce your grade if you don't use Roman numerals, capital letters, and Arabic numbers in the correct order. The point of the exercise is to get all the topics you want to include in your Web site into a list.

At this point in the process, you can use either paper and pencil or Word's Outline View to list the main points you want to present, with the subsidiary items you want to include under each one. The beginning of a Tree Fruit outline might look like this:

```
Fruit Trees
  Grafting and Pruning
  Apples
    Varieties
      Winesap, Cortland, Macintosh, etc
    Cider
      Pressing, fermenting, equipment
    Recipes
  Pears
    Cider
    Asian vs. European varieties
    Pear brandy
```

Mind maps A mind map adds a second dimension to the linear structure of an outline. To make a mind map, start with a blank sheet of paper, and write the main subject in the middle. Now write down the secondary topics around the main topic. Draw lines to show the connection from the main topic to the secondaries. Continue by adding all the other topics you want to include in your Web site, and add lines to show connections among them. The mind map in Figure 5.1 shows the beginning of the tree fruit Web site.

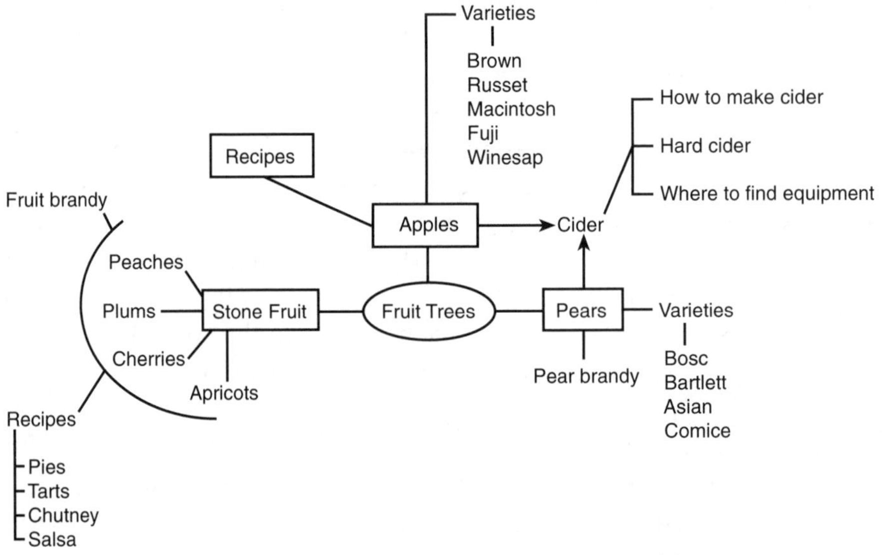

Figure 5.1 A mind map is a diagram that shows how things are related to one another.

Whether you're using an outline or a map, you should try to include everything that might be related to the main topic. Don't worry about duplicates or relative importance of different items—at this point, you just want to get everything down on paper. When you have finished your first draft of the outline or map, take another look and think about how you want to show each item in your Web site.

DIAGRAMMING YOUR WEB SITE

> A hidden connexion is stronger than an obvious one.
>
> Heraclitus
> *Fragments*, ~500 BC

The next step is to decide how best to organize the individual pages in your Web site.

Pyramid power

Figure 5.2 shows a Web site with a pyramid organization. Starting at the top, the home page has links to additional pages, each devoted to a particular type of fruit. Each of those pages has links to still other pages that contain information about a subject related to that fruit. From the Apples page, you can jump to a document about grafting and pruning your trees, a catalog of varieties, a list of recipes with jumps to individual items, and three separate pages devoted to squeezing and fermenting apple cider. There's also a page with links to other places on the Internet where you can find still more information about apples.

A pyramid structure is pretty simple—you start with a single page at the top and expand as you move down the pyramid. But when you finish with apples and move on to pears, it occurs to you that the information in the page about grafting and pruning applies to both types of fruit tree, so you add another link to an existing page. And because you can throw pears into your cider press, you create a link from pears to *that* page as well. By the time you figure out about peaches, plums, apricots, and nectarines, the diagram may look something like Figure 5.3. Your simple pyramid has begun to resemble a ball of yarn after an enthusiastic cat has attacked it for about half an hour. Add cherries and persimmons, and you may never find your way out.

Keep it simple.

Of course, Web sites don't all have to be that complicated. Some Web sites are simple and linear, like Figure 5.4, where each page has only one link to the next page in the sequence. Other sites treat the home page as a directory of services and place everything else one jump away, as in Figure 5.5.

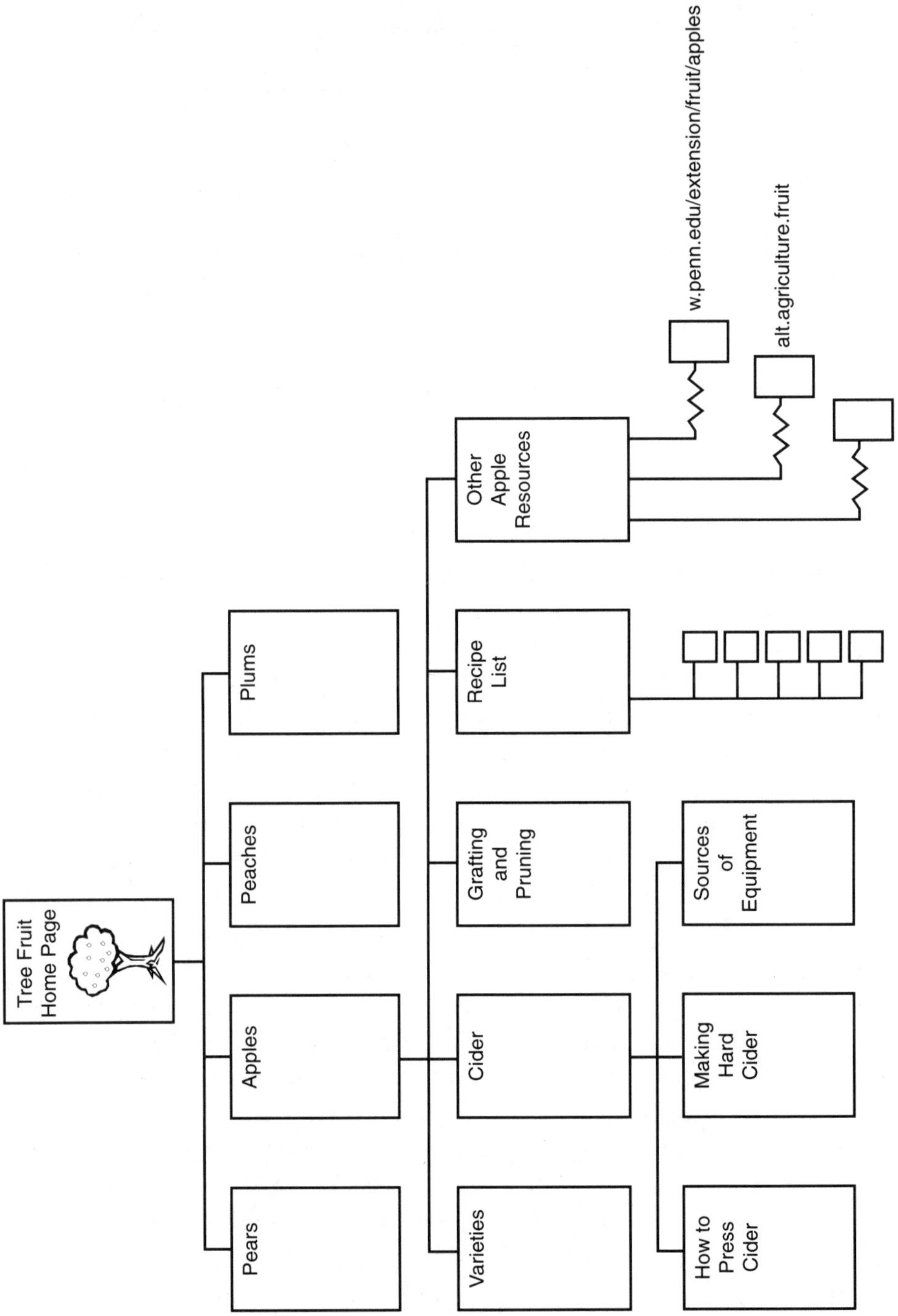

Figure 5.2 A Web site using pyramid organization resembles an upside-down tree.

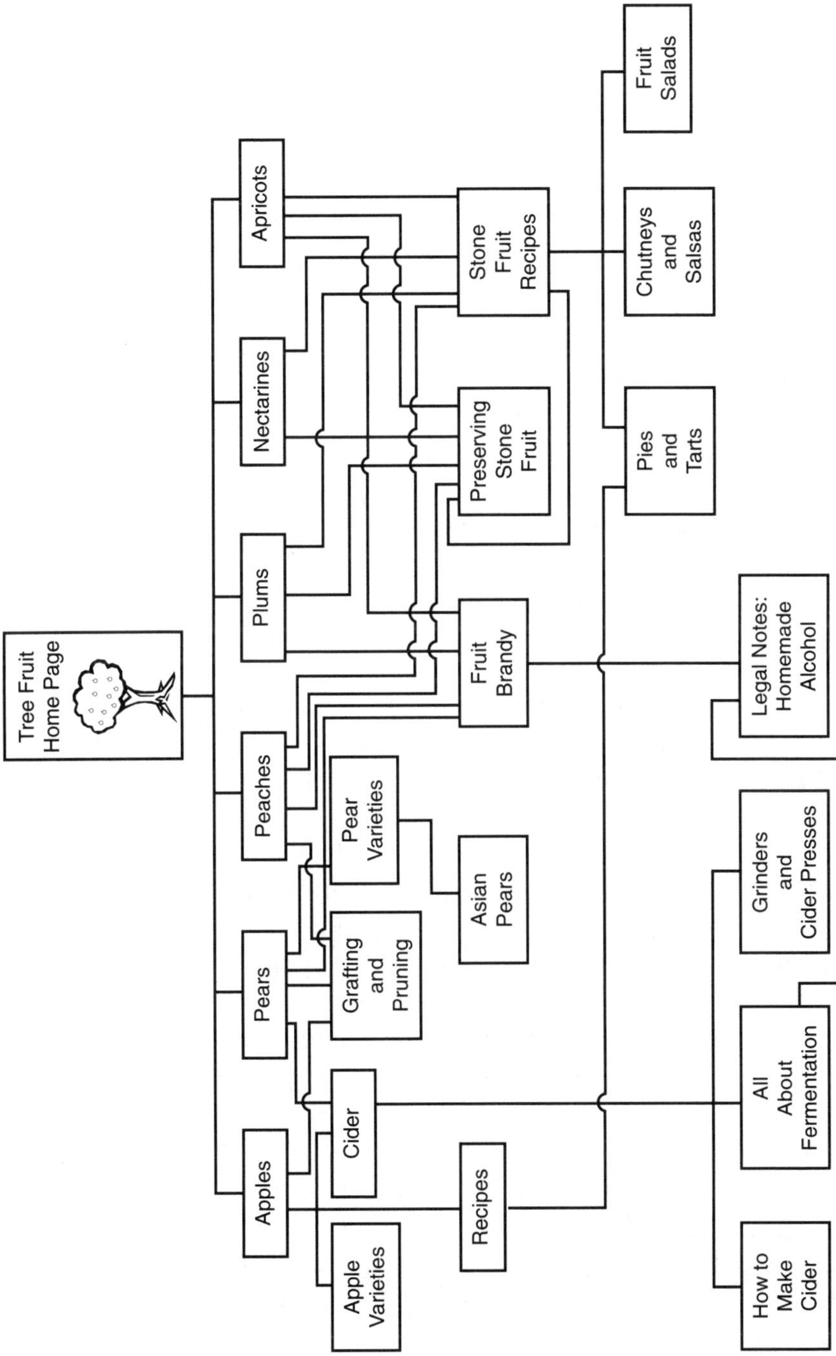

Figure 5.3 Add cross-references and interconnections, and things begin to get complicated.

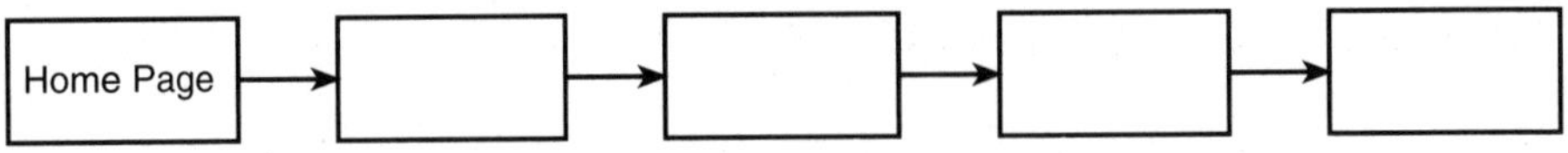

Figure 5.4 In a linear Web site, each page leads to the next.

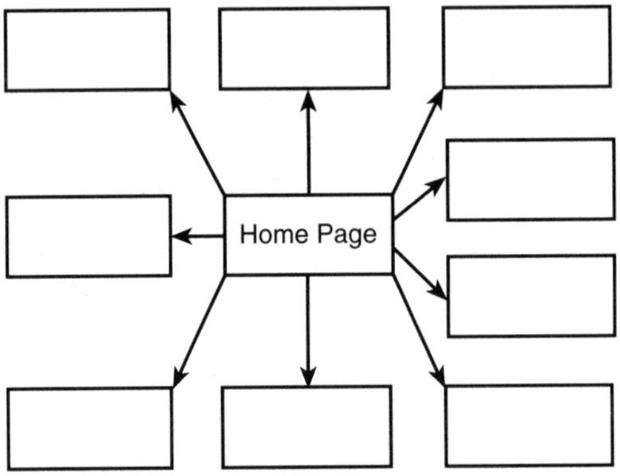

Figure 5.5 If your home page points to all the other pages, your site may resemble the spokes of a wheel.

In practice, your own site may end up as a combination of these and other arrangements. You might want to add links across branches of the pyramid, or some spokes might have two or three pages in a line or cross-links between related spokes. But the pyramid, line, and hub are the basic tools you should use to create your own structure.

If you're presenting anything more complicated than a linear set of pages, it will reduce your own confusion if you sketch out a diagram that shows how each page relates to the others. Once it's all on paper, you can easily trace the paths that a visitor to your site can follow. Since content is likely to change as you go along, you'll probably want to draw your diagram in pencil on graph paper, or use one of those erasable whiteboards. If you have any experience in computer programming, you will recognize this as the flowcharting stage.

A diagram is also useful if you are working with other people to design and build the site. Everybody involved can see the overall plan and where their own piece fits in. If you include a copy of the diagram when you submit your plan for approval, it will help convince the bosses or the client that you really know what you're doing.

DEFINING INDIVIDUAL PAGES

> We find little in a book but what we put there. But in great books, the mind finds room to put many things.
>
> Joseph Joubert
> *Pensées*, 1842

Use a worksheet.

Once you understand how your Web site will be organized, it's time to think about individual pages. If you're building a relatively simple site, you might be able to create pages directly from your diagram. In a more complicated site, however, you will want to make up a worksheet like the one in Figure 5.6 for each page.

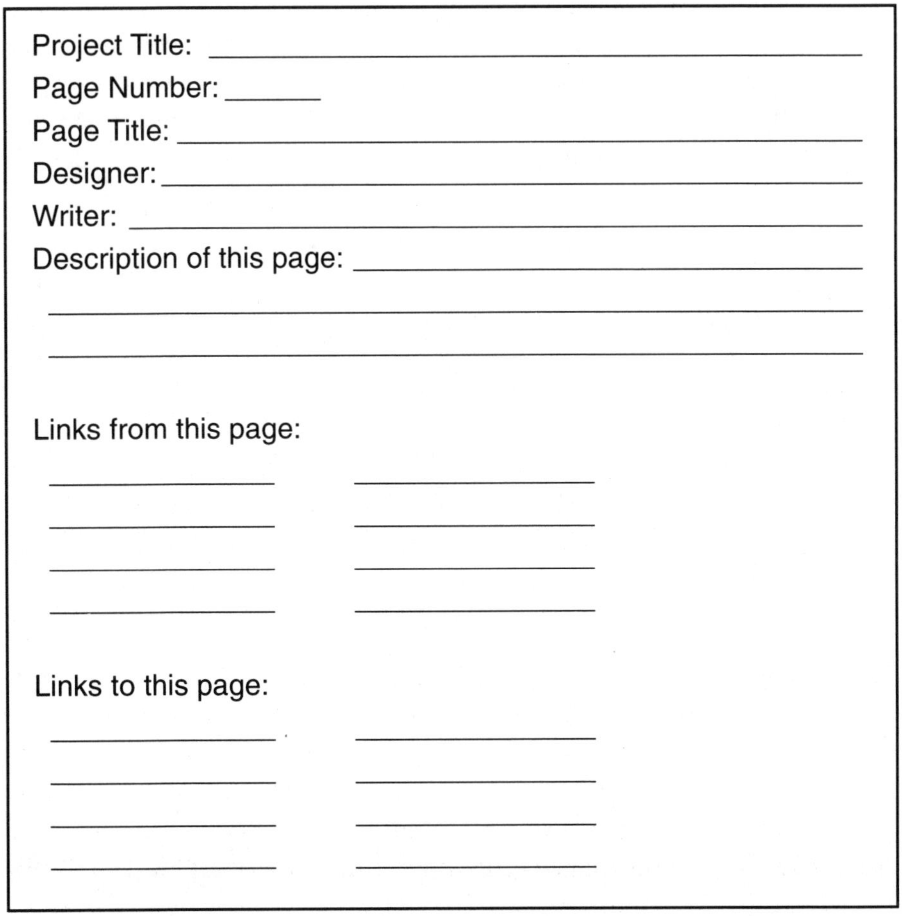
Project Title: ______
Page Number: ______
Page Title: ______
Designer: ______
Writer: ______
Description of this page: ______

Links from this page:

Links to this page:

Figure 5.6 Use a worksheet like this one for each page in your Web site.

If you want to use your computer to fill in the blanks, make a Word macro with the fields in the sample worksheet. If you plan to fill it in by hand, use Word to create a blank form and print or copy a worksheet for each Web page in your Web site diagram.

At this stage, you won't be able to fill in every space on the worksheet. As a start, you should complete the following fields for each page in your site:

- **Project Title**—The Project Title is the name that you or your organization use to identify the site. It may also be the title of the site's home page.
- **Page Number**—On a copy of your site diagram, assign a number to each page. You can number pages as 1, 2, 3, and so forth, or you can use some kind of complicated alphanumeric code, such as TF1(A) to identify the project and subject. It really doesn't matter how you number your pages as long as each page has a different identity from every other page.
- **Page Title**—The Page Title will probably be the top-level heading that appears on the page.
- **Description of This Page**—Write a sentence or two that describes the content of the page in this field.
- **Links from This Page**—If this page will include links to other pages, list the numbers of the pages in this site and the URLs of links to other places on the Internet.
- **Links to This Page**—If you know them, list the numbers of every page in this site that includes a link to this page. Except for your home page, every page must have at least one link from another page.

Don't worry about the HTML, Graphic Files, and HREF fields right now. You'll fill them in later.

As you've probably guessed, your stack of worksheets is really a catalog of the Web pages and other resources that you will assemble to create a Web site. When you start creating individual pages, you can use the worksheet for that page to make sure you haven't left out some essential element.

EVALUATING YOUR PLAN

> Next to sound judgement, diamonds and pearls are the rarest things in the world.
>
> Jean de La Bruyère
> "Of Opinions," *Characters,* 1688

This chapter has described the essential tools you need to start creating individual HTML pages. Before you start writing, you should take one more look at the plan and ask yourself these questions:

- Does this approach accomplish the goals of this project?
- Have you adequately covered the topic?
- Have you chosen the best type of organization for this information?
- Is there a path from the home page to every other page in the site?
- Have you identified all of the logical links between pages?

When you're satisfied with the answers to these questions, you're ready to start in on individual pages.

6 Creating HTML Documents: Formatting Text

> At what expense any valuable work is performed! At the expense of a life! If you do one thing well, what else are you good for in the meanwhile?
>
> Henry David Thoreau
> *Journal*, 1852

You have a general idea how your Web site will be organized, and you're ready to start creating individual pages. You have two choices: you can produce new pages from scratch or you can convert existing documents to HyperText Markup Language. We'll talk about attaching HTML formatting tags to text in this chapter; in Chapter 7, we'll add pictures and hypertext links.

HOW HTML WORKS

> Appearances are not held to be a clue to the truth. But we seem to have no other.
>
> Dame Ivy Compton-Burnett
> *Manservant and Maidservant*, 1947

HyperText Markup Language defines and labels each element of a document; when an HTML reader (such as a Web browser) recognizes a label, it uses a specific typeface, size, and style to display or print that element. Therefore, HTML itself only controls a document's structure, rather than the details of its appearance on your screen or on a page.

Why doesn't HTML assign more detail so a Web creator can have more control over a document? There are a couple of reasons. First,

HTML works on many platforms—a proper HTML page will look good (or at least make sense) on different kinds of monitors, computers, and operating systems rather than just a PC running Windows. If the design required umpteen different colors and typefaces, many users would not be able to display or print it. Second, HTML is designed to be compact in order to transfer it across the Internet as quickly as possible.

In the eye of the beholder

This is important: The same HTML document may look very different to people who use different browsers. As Figure 6.1 shows, a Web page that has lots of detail in, say, Netscape might be all scrunched up in Internet Assistant's browser. As you design and prepare your own HTML documents, you should concentrate on simple, clear structure rather than the appearance details in one or two browsers. As you read this chapter, remember: *HTML defines the* structure *of a document, not its appearance.*

Tags

As it moves across the Internet, an HTML document is pure ASCII text. All of the formatting information is contained in **tags**, which are enclosed in angle brackets, like this:

```
<BODY>
<H1>The Apple Cider Home Page</H1>
<P>
This is the World Wide Web's center for information about
making and drinking apple cider.
<H2>Apples for Cider</H2>
</BODY>
```

You should notice a couple of things in this example. First, HTML tags may be either upper- or lowercase letters. Internet Assistant writes tags in <CAPITALS>, but it and other browsers can also recognize tags in <lowercase> or <A Mixture of Both>. Second, HTML uses a start tag and an end tag for most text elements. The start tag contains the name of the tag, like this: <H1>. The end tag is the same name with a slash: </H1>. Think of the start tag as an instruction that says "everything from here until the end tag is this kind of text." When you tag a paragraph or a character string in Internet Assistant, you automatically add both a start tag and an end tag.

When a Web browser recognizes a tag embedded in a document, it consults a lookup table that tells it what that tag is supposed to do.

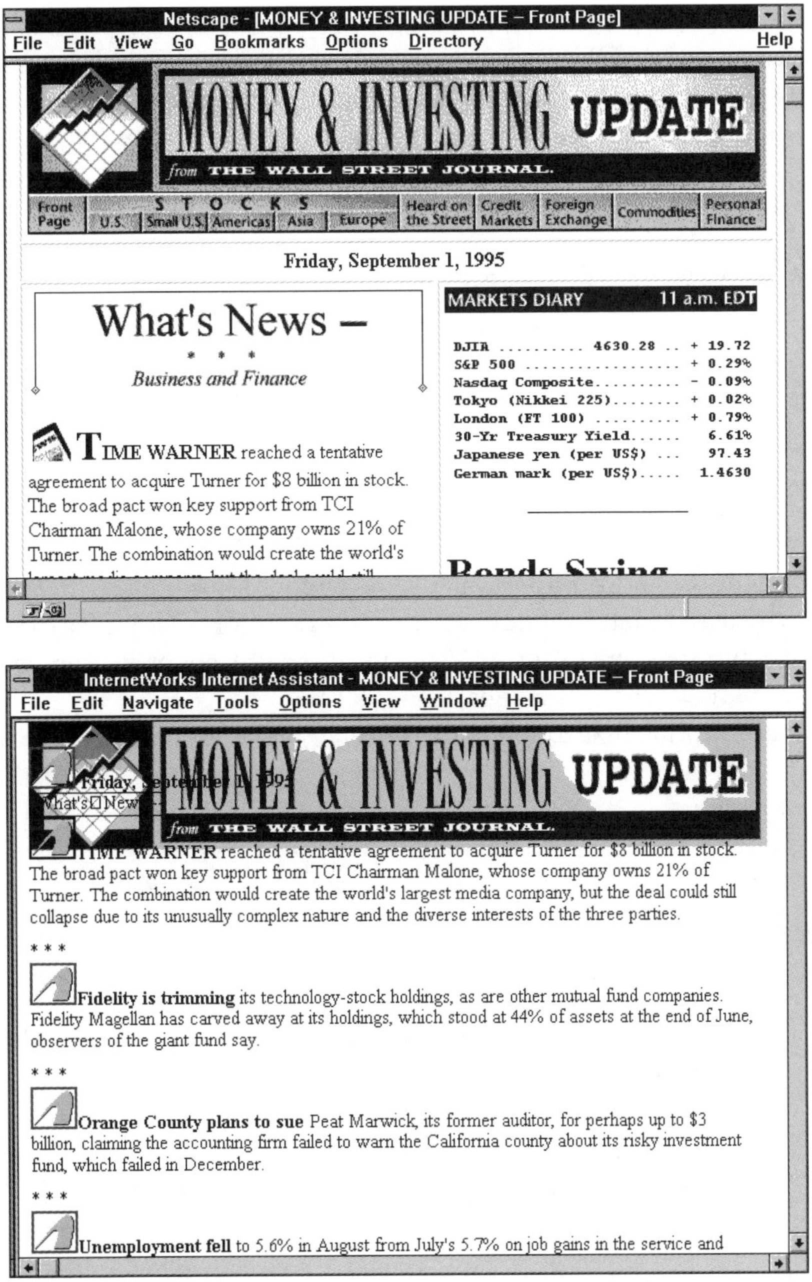

Figure 6.1 The same Web page in Netscape and Internet Assistant.

Depending on the browser, a tag may control the font, type size, and relative position of the tagged text. I say "depending on the browser" because some of them display all text in boring old ASCII characters.

One more thing about the way HTML deals with text: it ignores tabs, multiple spaces, and even carriage returns. Thus the following tags all look the same to HTML:

```
<H1>The Apple Cider Home Page</H1>

<H1>
The Apple Cider Home Page
</H1>

<H1>The Apple
Cider
Home Page</H1>
```

This would be more important if you were adding tags with a text editor instead of letting Internet Assistant do it for you. But since you might have to open up an HTML file to troubleshoot it, you really ought to know what these files can look like.

One important exception to the start tag/end tag rule is the <P> tag that HTML uses for plain text paragraphs. The latest HTML specifications include a </P> tag, but it's optional and Internet Assistant has opted not to use it.

STARTING A NEW PAGE

> "Chapter one, page one. Well, Lindsay, this isn't so difficult. Patrick, get me another drink. Let me see, where was I? What are you writing?"
>
> Agnes Gootch, reading back the beginnnings of Auntie Mame's dictated autobiography
>
> *Auntie Mame* (screenplay by Betty Comden and Adolph Green), 1958

As you read the rest of this chapter, you may want to follow along on your own PC by creating a dummy document. Here's what you need to do to open Word with the HTML editor active:

1. Start Word.

2. If you've installed Internet Assistant, you'll probably see a button at the left side of the formatting toolbar with a pair of eyeglasses. If it's not there, open the File menu and select the Templates command.
3. When the dialog box in Figure 6.2 appears, click on wordhtml.wll in the Global Templates and Add-ins list to place a checkmark in the box.

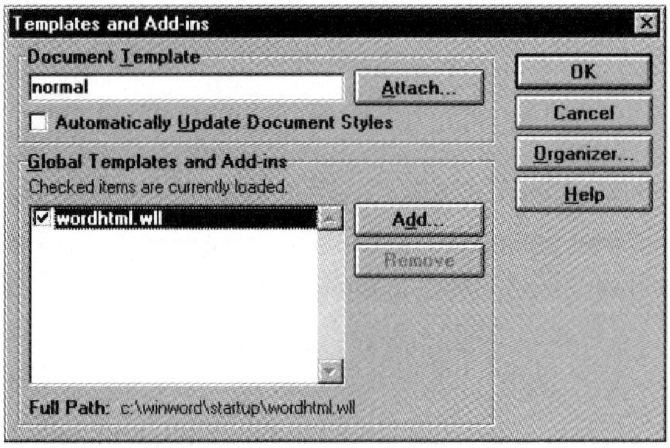

Figure 6.2 Select wordhtml.wll to add Internet Assistant to Word.

4. Once Internet Assistant is active, close the default DOCUMENT, and use the New command in the File menu to start a new document. Don't use the New button in the toolbar; it starts a conventional text document.
5. When you enter the New command, the New dialog box in Figure 6.3 appears. Select the Html template and click the OK button.

Figure 6.3 Select the Html template to create a new Web page.

Internet Assistant treats tags as paragraph styles in Word. Therefore, you can attach a tag to a paragraph by placing your cursor anywhere inside the paragraph and selecting the tag from the list in the style menu on the formatting toolbar. When you save the page as an HTML document (with an .htm file extension), Internet Assistant automatically adds all the necessary tags. Because the tags aren't in place until you save the document, the page may look somewhat different the next time you open the document in Word.

You should notice that some of the styles in the list appear in **boldface type**. When you select one of these styles, Internet Assistant attaches a tag to an entire paragraph. When you choose one of the styles whose name appears in the list in normal type, you apply that style to the currently selected text only.

ELEMENTS OF AN HTML DOCUMENT

> Everything is worthy of notice, for everything can be interpreted.
>
> Carl Gustav Jung
> *Modern Man in Search of a Soul*, 1933

It's elemental. Every HTML document is supposed to contain certain standard items. Some don't include all of them, and most browsers are smart enough to ignore the fact that some elements are missing. However, Internet Assistant automatically adds these tags to all documents. The bare framework of an HTML document created in Internet Assistant looks like this:

```
<HTML>
<HEAD>
<TITLE>The Title of the Document</TITLE>
</HEAD>
<BODY>
   .
   .
   .
This area contains the content of the document.
   .
   .
   .
</BODY>
</HTML>
```

Notice that the tags are **nested**; the <HTML>...</HTML> tags enclose everything in the document, and the <HEAD>...</HEAD> and <BODY>...</BODY> tags also surround text that is itself identified with a tag. Internet Assistant inserts the <HTML>, <HEAD>, and <BODY> tags automatically.

THE DOCUMENT HEAD

> So the heart be right, it is no matter which way the head lies.
>
> Sir Walter Raleigh
> At his execution, when asked which way he preferred to lay his head, 1618

The information in the <HEAD> section of the document does not appear when a browser displays it. The document head contains the title, and it may also include some other reference information. For every new document, Internet Assistant automatically creates a head, which includes elements that identify the name of the person who created the document and the program that person used (e.g., Internet Assistant).

Use your head.

The title is the only absolutely essential element of a document head. The title may appear in hot lists, title bars, and other descriptions of the document, and many Internet search tools examine document titles when they're looking for Web pages related to a specific topic. Therefore, your title should actually describe the contents of the page. For example, "Apple Varieties for Cider" is a good title, but "My Favorite Varieties" or "My Home Page" are not because they don't give a reader enough information about the content.

The HTML specification says that a title may have up to 64 characters (including letters, spaces, and punctuation marks), but if you can hold the title to no more than about half a dozen words, you will have a better chance of fitting it all into title bars and hot lists. For example, Figure 6.4 shows a list of Favorites in Microsoft Internet Explorer. Notice that the titles of two out of the four entries are too long to fit in the menu.

To assign a title to a document, use the HTML Document Info command in Word's File menu and type the title in the Document Head Information dialog shown in Figure 6.5.

Figure 6.4 Two of these items have long titles.

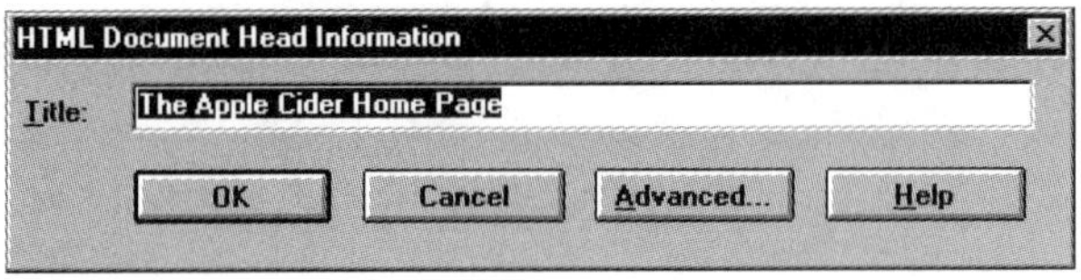

Figure 6.5 Type the title in the Document Head Information dialog.

The Advanced button opens additional dialog boxes that you can use to add more items to the document head, but you can generally ignore them. They're there for information purposes, but they don't actually affect the appearance or performance of the document.

THE DOCUMENT BODY

> I sing the body electric.
>
> Walt Whitman
> *Leaves of Grass*, 1855

The text and other elements that actually appear in a Web page or other HTML document are all surrounded by the <BODY>...</BODY> tags.

Headings

Headings in HTML documents are like headlines and subheads on a magazine or book page; they make the text easier to read by breaking it up into smaller pieces and providing the reader with a hint about the subject of each piece.

Typically the top-level heading is used as a main title for the page. It may be exactly the same as the <TITLE> in the document head, or a shorter version of that title. Since many Web pages contain more information than will fit in a single screen, the top-level heading should be at the top of the document.

Six heads are better than one.

HTML recognizes six levels of headings, which use the tags <H1> through <H6>. Most Web browsers display each type of heading in a progressively less prominent form. So, for example, <H1> might be 18-point bold, <H2> 16-point, <H3> 14-point, and so forth. Therefore, you could use <H1> as your main title, <H2> as the most important level of headline, and <H3> through <H6> as progressively less important levels of subhead. In Figure 6.6, "The Apple Cider Home Page" is Heading 1, "Apples for Cider" is Heading 2, and "Growing Cider Apples" is Heading 3.

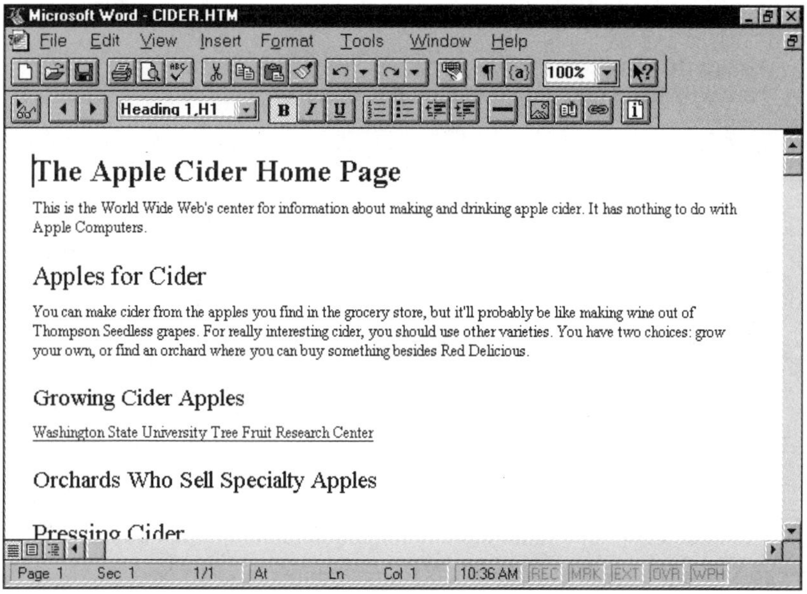

Figure 6.6 Headings in Internet Assistant.

To create a heading with Internet Assistant, type the text of the heading in the body of the document as a separate paragraph and use the drop-down style menu in the formatting toolbar to assign a heading number. Remember that the document does not specify the actual font and size, so the display you see in Word is arbitrary. Many readers will see the text quite differently from the way you see it in Word.

As a general rule, you should treat headings like items in an outline: use lower level headings under higher level headings, and don't skip a level. Your page might organized like this:

```
Heading 1
Heading 2
Heading 3
Heading 3
Heading 2
Heading 3
```

If it's easier to visualize, you can indent each heading level, like this:

```
Heading 1
  Heading 2
    Heading 3
    Heading 3
  Heading 2
    Heading 3
```

Because browsers ignore tabs and indents, all of these headings will remain flush left in the actual Web page, but indenting them might make it easier to work with as you enter your text.

Don't be surprised if your page looks different after you save it and reopen it. Internet Assistant converts Word styles to HTML tags when you save a document, and it applies those tags when you open the document.

Body Text

HTML identifies body text with Paragraph tags. To be consistent with other Word styles, Internet Assistant calls this "Normal" style and treats it as the default. If you don't attach any other style to a paragraph, Internet Assistant saves that paragraph with a <P> tag.

Lists

I've got a little list.

You could create a list in an HTML document using nothing but headings and body text, but the document might look more interesting if you use one or more of the list tags that you can add with Internet Assistant. There are several different kinds of lists:

- Numbered lists
- Bulleted lists
- Directory lists
- Menu lists
- Definition lists
- Indented lists

A list must include start and end tags for the entire list, as well as individual tags for each item in the list. Internet Assistant adds these tags automatically when you identify a series of paragraphs as a list.

Most lists are of short items, such as names of people or things, but if it's appropriate to the content of your page, you could also format a series of short paragraphs as a list.

Numbered Lists

One, two, three...

As the name suggests, a numbered list is a list in which the items appear in a specific order, and each item has a number. A numbered list begins and ends with an <OL> (for Ordered List) tag, and each item in the list begins with an <LI> (List Item) tag. A numbered list is good for step-by-step procedures, and for other lists in which the order or number of items in the list is important. Figure 6.7 shows a numbered list.

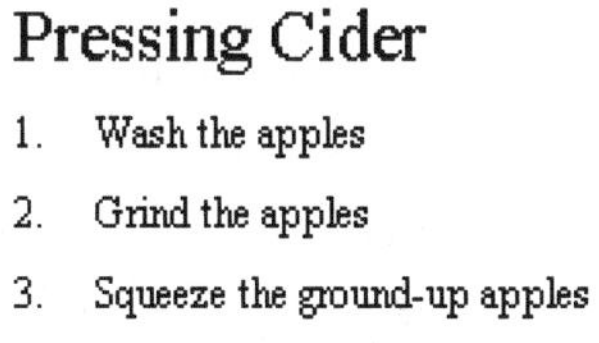

Figure 6.7 A numbered list.

You can create a numbered list in Internet Assistant in two ways:

1. Type each item in the list as a separate paragraph. Don't assign numbers to the individual items.

The Numbered List button

2. Select the entire list and click on the Numbered List button in the formatting toolbar, or if you prefer, you can use the Numbering command in the Format menu instead.

Bulleted Lists

In an unordered list, the order in which the items appear is less important. Many browsers put a bullet at the beginning of each item in an unordered list, so Internet Assistant calls them "bulleted lists." The HTML tag for unordered lists is <UL>, with the same <LI> tag for each list item. Figure 6.8 shows a bulleted list.

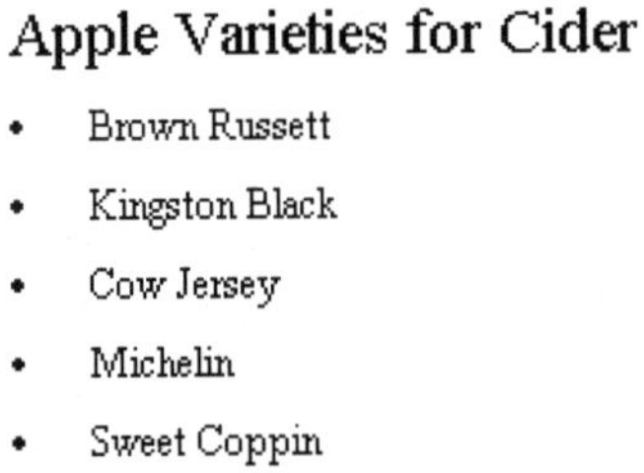

Figure 6.8 A bulleted list.

Creating a bulleted list is very similar to creating a numbered list. Use the Bulleted List button in the formatting toolbar or the Bullets command in the Format menu to tag a paragraph, or assign the tag first and then type the list items.

Directory Lists

Internet Assistant shows directory lists in three columns, but Netscape and some other browsers show them as one column, with each item bulleted. Since you should try to preserve what little control is possible over the layout of your Web pages, it's probably a good idea to avoid using directory lists at all. Figure 6.9 shows a directory list as it appears in Internet Assistant.

You can to type a directory list in two ways:

1. Put each item in a separate paragraph.
2. Type three items in each paragraph, with a tab between each pair of items.

Apple Varieties for Cider

Brown Russett	Kingston Black	Cow Jersey
Michelin	Sweet Coppin	Chisel Jersey

Figure 6.9 A directory list.

Either way, when you save the document, Internet Assistant will tag each item separately. To attach tags to a directory, choose the Directory,DIR item in the formatting toolbar style menu.

Menu Lists

A menu is still another way to show a list of items in a Web page. Some browsers display menu lists differently from body text, but others simply show them as a series of paragraphs. Internet Assistant and Netscape show menus as bulleted lists, whereas Internet Explorer displays them as indented lists without bullets.

Definition Lists

As the name suggests, a definition list is a list of words or phrases, with an explanation of each one. Internet Assistant can add two kinds of definitions—Definition List (<DL>) and Definition Compact (<DL COMPACT>). Figure 6.10 shows a definition list.

Apple Varieties for Cider

Brown Russett	A good, all-purpose apple that produces slightly spicy juice
Kingston Black	Slightly tannic, but good for a varietal hard cider
Cow Jersey	Extremely bitter
Michelin	Green and acidic
Sweet Coppin	Bitter sweet
Chisel Jersey	Bitter sharp

Figure 6.10 A definition list in Internet Assistant.

Internet Assistant displays terms and their definitions on the same line, but many other browsers indent the definition on the next line. Figure 6.11 shows the same definition list in Netscape.

Apple Varieties for Cider

Brown Russett
  A good, all-purpose apple that produces slightly spicy juice
Kingston Black
  Slightly tannic, but good for a varietal hard cider
Cow Jersey
  Extremely bitter
Michelin
  Green and acidic
Sweet Coppin
  Bitter sweet
Chisel Jersey
  Bitter sharp

Figure 6.11 The same definition list in Netscape.

Definition Compact is not supported in many browsers. It is supposed to squeeze the term and the definition closer together, but since it will probably look just like a normal definition list, you shouldn't bother with it.

Definition terms begin with a <DT> tag and definitions begin with a <DD> tag, but Internet Assistant adds the tags to your text automatically when it converts your document to HTML. To create a definition list:

1. Type the term, a tab, and then the definition, all in a single paragraph, like this:

   ```
   Term [Tab] Definition [Enter]
   ```

2. Select all the terms and definitions you have typed
3. Choose the Definition List,DL from the drop-down style menu.

Indented Lists

We know that browsers ignore spaces in HTML; if you want to show an indented list in a Web page, you must nest one list within another list. Using HTML tags, the structure looks like this:

```
<OL>
<LI>French Apples
  <UL>
  <LI>Michelin
```

```
  <LI>Belle de Boskoop
  </UL>
<LI>English Apples
  <UL>
  <LI>Harry Masters
  <LI>Cow Jersey
  </UL>
<LI>American Apples
  <UL>
  <LI>Esopus Spitzenberg
  <LI>New York State #643
  </UL>
</OL>
```

Indenting is a lot easier with Internet Assistant:

1. Type the list.
2. Attach the List Bullet or List Number tags to each item.
3. Select the ones you want to indent.
4. Use the Increase Indent command on the formatting toolbar or the Format menu.

The Increase Indent button

Figure 6.12 shows the nested list.

Figure 6.12 A nested list in a Web page.

Horizontal Lines

Most graphic elements in Web pages have to be imported into the document from separate image files. However, it is possible to add a horizontal line with the <HR> (horizontal rule) tag. That's why you see so many horizontal lines like the one in Figure 6.13 in Web pages.

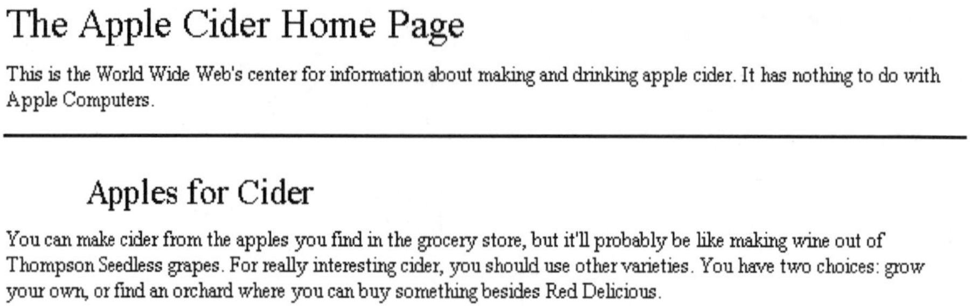
The Apple Cider Home Page

This is the World Wide Web's center for information about making and drinking apple cider. It has nothing to do with Apple Computers.

Apples for Cider

You can make cider from the apples you find in the grocery store, but it'll probably be like making wine out of Thompson Seedless grapes. For really interesting cider, you should use other varieties. You have two choices: grow your own, or find an orchard where you can buy something besides Red Delicious.

Figure 6.13 A horizontal line.

Horizontal rules do a good job of separating major sections of a Web page, but because they're so easy to add, many HTML designers use them too much. Include horizontal lines where they improve the look of your document, but don't overdo it.

Block Quotes

If you include a quotation in your Web page as a separate paragraph, consider using the Blockquote tag to set it off from the rest of your text. In most browsers, a block quote is indented or otherwise set apart from other text.

Preformatted Text

Sometimes you may want to include a table or other text in your HTML document in a specific layout. Since HTML normally ignores spaces, tabs, and returns, you need a special tag that includes the formatting along with the text. When you assign the Preformatted,PRE style to a paragraph, the tagged text will include all of the tabs, spaces, line breaks, and carriage returns that were in the original.

To maintain the same spacing in any kind of page display, preformatted text is limited to nonproportional typefaces that make the text look like it came out of an old typewriter.

If your table or other preformatted text is more than about 60 characters wide, you should use the PRE WIDE style, which squeezes the text into narrower, but still ugly, monospaced type.

Addresses

Credit (or blame) where credit is due

It's common practice to add the e-mail address of the person who created a Web site to the bottom of the home page so readers know where to contact the creator. Some experts even recommend that you put your address on every page. (See Figure 6.14.) Because the address is separate from the content of most pages, a horizontal line just above the address serves to create a visual break between the address and the rest of the page. The Address tag command is in the drop-down style menu.

---

winesap@cider.org

J. Appleseed, webmaster

Figure 6.14 An address at the bottom of a Web page.

The bottom of the document is also a good place for copyright notices, the page's creation date, and other boilerplate information that isn't directly related to the content of the page.

CHANGING THE TEXT

> Look twice, if you want a just conception; look once, if what you want is a sense of beauty.
>
> Henri Frédéric Amiel
> *Journal,* 1852

HTML doesn't specify the appearance of a block of text, but it does allow you to attach special tags to a character, word or phrase that the browser will recognize as a signal to display it differently from the normal text. Most browsers show text marked with many of these tags with a variation on the fonts they use for standard body text, such as bold or italic versions of the same font.

Type formats

There are two kinds of character styles. **Physical styles** are the kind of variation on the normal type style that you use in other Word documents—**boldface**, *italic,* and underlined. You attach tags for this kind of formatting just as you would if you were creating a paper document, with buttons in the formatting toolbar or keyboard commands like Ctrl+B and Ctrl+I. Two other physical styles are in the style menu: ~~strikethrough~~ and `Typewriter`.

The other kind of character style is a little less obvious. **Logical styles** work like the paragraph styles we explained earlier in this chapter: when a browser encounters one, it goes to a lookup table to figure out how to display it. To attach a logical style tag, select the text you want to change, and choose the style you want from the drop-down menu in the formatting toolbar.

There are eight possible character styles:

1. **Emphasis <EM>**—As you would expect, the <EM> tag is used for type that should appear with some kind of visual emphasis. Browsers usually display emphasized text in italics.
2. **Strong <STRONG>**—Strong text is even more prominent than emphasized text. It usually appears in boldface type.
3. **Code <CODE>**—The Code style is used for samples of computer code. It usually appears in monospace type.
4. **Sample <SAMP>**—The Sample style is another way to display computer code. It also appears as monospace type.
5. **Keyboard <KBD>**—The Keyboard style is used for text that the reader should enter into a computer. Like <CODE> and <SAMP>, it usually appears as monospace type.
6. **Variable <VAR>**—A variable is a piece of text that shows where the reader should insert the word, characters, or phrase that applies to the specific situation, such as *yourname*. It's usually shown as italics or underlined text.
7. **Cite <CITE>**—A citation typically appears at the end of a quotation to show its source.
8. **Definition <DFN>**—A definition tag is sometimes used to identify a new term when it first appears. It may appear on a Web page in italics or boldface. The word **definition** in this sentence is an example of this kind of usage.

MANUALLY ADDING HTML TAGS

> The test of a vocation is the love of the drudgery it involves.
>
> Logan Pearsall Smith
> *Afterthoughts*, 1931

Adding tags by hand

Internet Assistant includes commands or styles that can add all of the standard HTML tags to a document, but it's also possible to insert an HTML tag directly into your document. You might want to do this for several reasons. You may want to include one of the nonstandard tags that are supported by some, but not all browsers. The next version of the HTML specification will probably include some new formats. You might want to add a Meta tag that contains a hidden comment that will not appear in the document itself.

For example, Netscape recognizes a <CENTER> tag that places text in the center of the line. Some other browser developers have followed Netscape's lead, but others ignore this tag and continue to start all text on the right margin. You can't automatically add a <CENTER> tag with Internet Assistant, but since Netscape accounts for more than 70 percent of all hits on many popular Web sites, you might decide that centering your headings is a good idea. Don't forget the </CENTER> tag at the end of the heading. In Internet Assistant 2.0, you can find CENTER in the menu of styles.

Inserting Formatting Tags

To add an HTML tag to the body of your document, follow these steps:

1. Place your cursor at the exact location where you want the new tag.
2. Use the HTML Markup command in the Insert menu to open the dialog box in Figure 6.15.

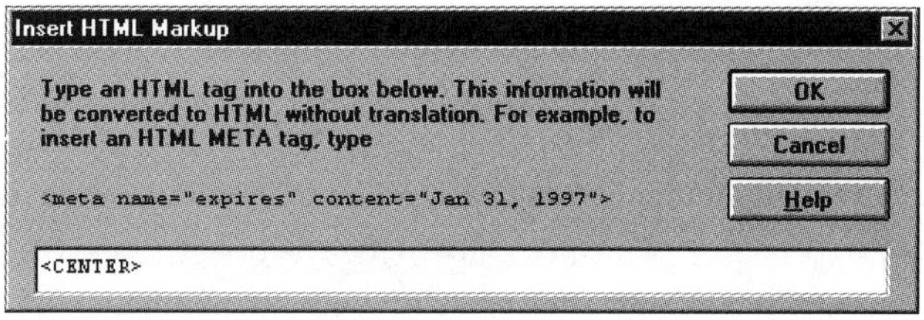

Figure 6.15 The Insert HTML Markup dialog box.

3. Type the exact text of the tag, including the opening and closing brackets.
4. Click the OK button.

Word displays the new tag as <<HTML Markup>>. To see the content of the tag, double-click on it. If you save the document and reopen it in Edit view, Word displays an <<Unknown HTML Tag>> label every time it finds a tag it does not recognize.

Adding Meta Tags to the Document Head

You might also want to include one or more nonprinting **Meta tags** in the document head to add reference or document control information to the source code. Meta tags are visible when you display the document as source code, but they are ignored by Web browsers. If you're using the Project Worksheet I recommended in Chapter 5, you could place your internal project number or page number in a Meta tag.

Here's the procedure:

1. Open the File menu and select the HTML Document Info command.
2. Click the Advanced button in the Document Head Information dialog box.
3. Click the Meta button to open the Insert HTML Markup dialog box. This is the same dialog box you just used to add a formatting tag.
4. The first word in the tag must be "META." Type the text that you want to add to your source code, beginning and ending with angle brackets. For example, <META Project No. 6SJ6GT Page 3>.

CONVERTING FROM A WORD DOCUMENT TO HTML

> Change is not made without inconvenience, even from worse to better.
>
> Samuel Johnson
> Preface to *A Dictionary of the English Language*, 1755

Converting Word docs

Up until now, we've assumed that you are creating a new Web page from scratch, but that's not always the case. Sometimes, you may want to take an existing paper document and put it up on the World Wide Web or an internal network for online distribution.

That's one of the strengths of Internet Assistant. If the original document was produced in Word, or in a format that you can convert to Word, it's relatively simple to convert it to HTML. Internet Assistant automatically converts styles in other style sheets to the styles that the Html template recognizes.

What's missing?

Converting is relatively simple, but it's not perfect; you're likely to lose a lot of formatting and layout elements that were included in the original. In particular, HTML will not recognize:

- Annotations
- Borders and shading
- Captions
- Embedded objects, including equations, clip art, Word art, and MS Draw objects
- Footnotes and endnotes
- Frames
- Headers and footers
- Indented paragraphs, except in <OL> and <UL> lists
- Index entries
- Page breaks and section breaks
- Revision marks
- Tabs, except in <PRE> and <DL> paragraphs
- Table of Contents entries

Of course, losing many of these elements won't make any difference because they don't apply to Web pages.

Here's what you need to do to run a conversion:

1. Open the document.
2. If the original document was not formatted, run the AutoFormat command from the Format menu.
3. Enter the Save As command in the File menu.

4. Scroll down to HyperText Markup Language (HTML) in the Save File As Type box and select it as the file type.
5. Type the filename with an .htm file extension. Click the OK button.

If you're converting from a document that uses anything but the Normal style sheet, you must create a translation map that takes specific styles in the original and changes them to HTML styles. To do this, you must add a line in the [STYLEMAP] section of the \windows\wordhtml.ini file for every style you want to convert. The format is **original_style=HTML Tag**.

Unless you're converting a lot of documents, adding conversion commands to the .ini file may be more trouble than it's worth. It's probably quicker and easier to just convert the document to HTML and use the commands in the formatting bar to reformat each paragraph.

DISPLAYING HTML TAGS

> An old tutor of a college said to one of his pupils: Read over your compositions, and whenever you meet with a passage which you think is particularly fine, strike it out.
>
> Samuel Johnson
> quoted in *The Life of Samuel Johnson* by James Boswell, 1791

Viewing tags You can get a rough idea how your HTML document will look in a browser by saving the document with a .htm file extension, closing it, and reopening it in Word. But sometimes it's even more useful to look at the HTML source code, including the document head and all the tags. Here's the way to do it:

1. Save the document.
2. Close the document.
3. Select the Open command in the File menu.
4. Find and select the name of the document you want to view.
5. Click on the box next to Confirm Conversions in the lower right corner of the dialog box. There should be an X in the box. Click the OK button.

6. When the Convert File dialog box appears, select Text Only and click the OK button.

The source code will appear as a Word document. You can edit the text and manually add or remove tags, but you can't use any of Internet Assistant's formatting tools. Therefore, it's a good idea to treat this as a read-only document.

To return to HTML format, close the document and reopen it, but this time turn off the Confirm Conversions option in the Open dialog box.

Up to this point, we've covered the "Markup Language" part of HTML, but it's still just a formatting method that doesn't supply as many details as most other Word styles. Chapter 7 explains how to add hypertext links to your document.

7 Creating HTML Documents: Hypertext Links and Graphics

Wonder . . . and not any expectation of advantage from its discoveries, is the first principle which prompts mankind to the study of Philosophy, of that science which pretends to lay open the concealed connections that unite the various appearances of nature.

Adam Smith
The History of Astronomy, 1795

So far, we've talked about using Internet Assistant to create HTML pages that are all text; but the whole point of HTML is **hypertext**—the links that carry a reader from one document to another. And, as you know if you've spent any time at all exploring the World Wide Web, most pages include at least one picture or other graphic element. These graphics are not part of the HTML document itself, but HTML uses a special kind of link to tell a browser where to find graphic images and where to place them on the page. This chapter explains how to add both kinds of links to an HTML document.

LINKS IN HTML DOCUMENTS

The web, then, or the pattern; a web at once sensuous and logical, an elegant and pregnant texture: that is style, that is the foundation of the art of literature.

Robert Louis Stevenson
The Art of Writing, 1885

Another link in the chain

A **link** is an instruction in an HTML document that carries a reader to a new document or other file, or to another part of the same document.

In most browsers, a link is a word or phrase that appears in a special color or type style (or both), or a picture with a special border. When the reader selects the link, the browser opens the target file or moves to the target location in the current file. A hypertext link tag begins with the code HREF=.

Types of Links

There are three types of links:

- Relative links
- URL (Uniform Resource Locator) links
- Anchor links

Relative links

Everything is relative.

A relative link specifies a destination on the same system as the HTML document that contains the original link. Most relative links are in the same subdirectory or folder, but they could be in a different directory, or even a different drive on the same computer. The path of a relative link may itself be relative to the current HTML document file or an "absolute link" that specifies the complete path name that begins with the disk drive letter or the top-level subdirectory. For example, consider the following directory:

```
                c:
                |
             \apples
                |
   ┌────────────┼─────────────────┐
   |            |                 |
cider.htm   orchards.htm      \winesap
                                  |
                              growers.htm
```

If the current HTML document is cider.htm, located in your c:\apples directory, which also contains orchards.htm and a subdirectory called winesap, HREF="orchards.htm" is a relative link to a file in the same file as the document that contains the link. HREF="winesap/growers.htm" is a relative link to a file in the winesap subdirectory, which is in the same directory as the current URL. Notice that the separators are the forward slashes used in UNIX rather than DOS-type backslashes, even though you're using DOS and Windows.

On the other hand, HREF="/apples/orchards.htm" or even HREF="/c:/apples/orchards.htm" would be an absolute link.

As a general rule, the best way to handle relative links is to place all the files to which you have links in the same directory as the original document file, or in subdirectories under the original directory, to avoid using absolute links. If you ever have to move your Web site to a different Web server (and you will, unless you have a permanent Internet connection to your PC), it will be a great deal easier if you don't have to change a lot of absolute links that point to the directory structure of a different computer.

URL Links

URL (Uniform Resource Locator) links include the full Internet address and path of the target file. For example, if you want to include a link to the home page at Washington State University's Tree Fruit Research Center, you might have a link that looks like this: HREF="http://mtvernon.wazzu.edu/trees.HTML".

Anchor Links

Raising anchors

An **anchor** is a specific location within a document that may be the destination of a link. A link to an anchor may be either a relative link or a URL. Anchors are identified within a document with a NAME tag. Internet Assistant uses bookmarks to create anchors.

Creating a Bookmark

Bookmarks

A **bookmark** identifies a specific destination for an anchor link. You can use anchor links and bookmarks to add jumps within the same document, or links to a particular piece of information in another document. A bookmark may be either a specific insertion point, or a word, phrase, or graphic element. For example, you might put a summary at the top of a long document, with links to other parts of the document where a reader can find more details about the items in the summary. Another common use of anchor links is a "return to top" link at the end of a document that fills more than a single screen.

Bookmarks are not visible when you view a document in a browser. Unlike links, which most browsers display in a contrasting color, bookmarks don't show up on the reader's screen.

To add a bookmark to a document, follow these steps:

1. Place the cursor at the insertion point where you want to place your bookmark, or select a string of text.

The Bookmark button

2. Click on the Bookmark button in the formatting toolbar, or open the Edit menu and select the Bookmark command.
3. When the Bookmark dialog box shown in Figure 7.1 appears, type the name you want to use for this bookmark in the Name field, or choose one of the names from the list, and click the Add button.

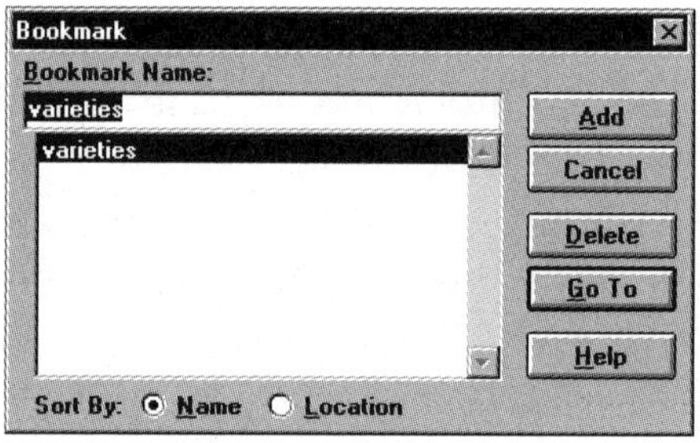

Figure 7.1 The Bookmark dialog box.

Adding Links in Internet Assistant

The HyperLink button

To insert a link to an HTML document in Word, choose an insertion point or select the text you want to use as the link, and either click the HyperLink button in the formatting toolbar or open the Insert menu and choose the HyperLink command. When the HyperLink <A> dialog box appears, choose the tab that describes the type of link you want: to a local document, a URL, or a bookmark.

Link to a Local Document

Local links

Choose the Local Document tag if the destination of this link is a file on the same computer as the current document, or another computer on the same LAN. The Local Document tab in Figure 7.2 includes the fields described in the following list.

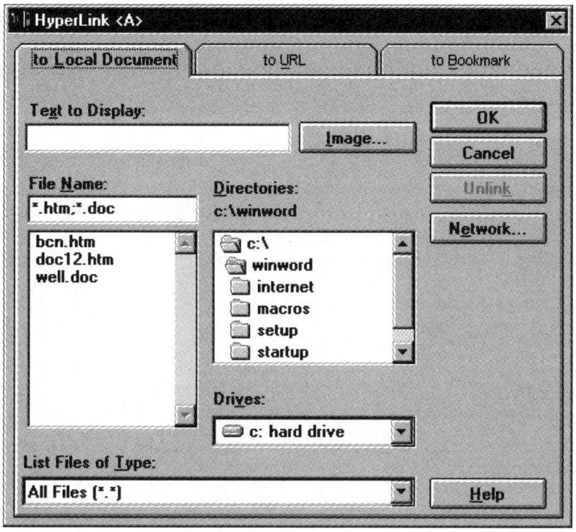

Figure 7.2 The HyperLink to Local Document tab.

- Text to Display—If you selected a word or phrase when you entered the HyperLink command, that word or phrase will appear in the Text to Display field. Any additions, deletions, or changes you make to the text in the field will also appear in your document.
- Image—To use a picture or other graphic element as your link, click the Image button and choose the image file from the file selector in the Insert Picture dialog box.
- File Selector—Use the File Name menu and the lists of directories and drives to find the file that you want to use as a destination for this link. You can use the drop-down List Files of Type menu at the bottom of the HyperLink <A> Local Document dialog box to limit your search to certain file types, or to search All Files.
- Network—If your PC is connected to a LAN, you can create a link to a file on another computer on the same LAN by clicking the Network button.
- Unlink—The Unlink button removes the hyperlink tag and returns the link to default paragraph font format.

Click the OK button to create the link.

Link to a URL

Use the URL tag to create a link to a file located someplace else on the Internet. Figure 7.3 shows the URL tab.

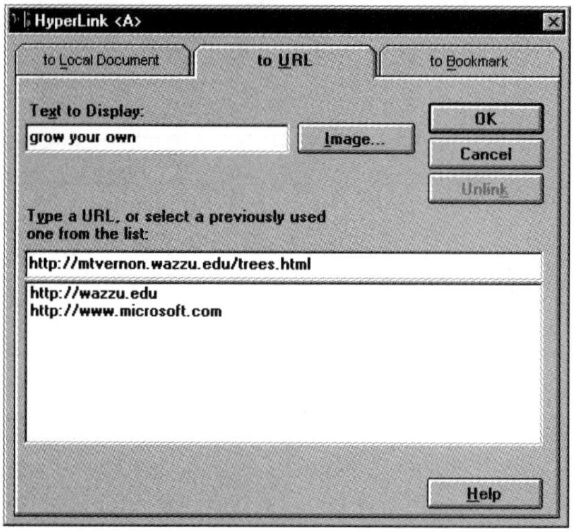

Figure 7.3 The HyperLink to URL tab.

Once again, the Text to Display field shows the word or phrase that will appear as this link. To use a picture as the link, click the Image button.

If you have used the same URL as a link before, it will appear in the list at the bottom of this dialog box. You can select a URL from the list or enter a new URL in the Type a URL field. Click the OK button to create the link.

Link to a Bookmark

A link to a bookmark takes a user to an anchor (which Internet Assistant calls a bookmark) at a specific place within the current document. To create an anchor link, choose the Bookmark tab to display the dialog box in Figure 7.4.

By now, the routine for defining a link is familiar. If you want a link from a word or phrase, the text of the link appears in the Text to Display field; for a link from a picture, click the Image button. Select a bookmark from the list to associate the link with a destination.

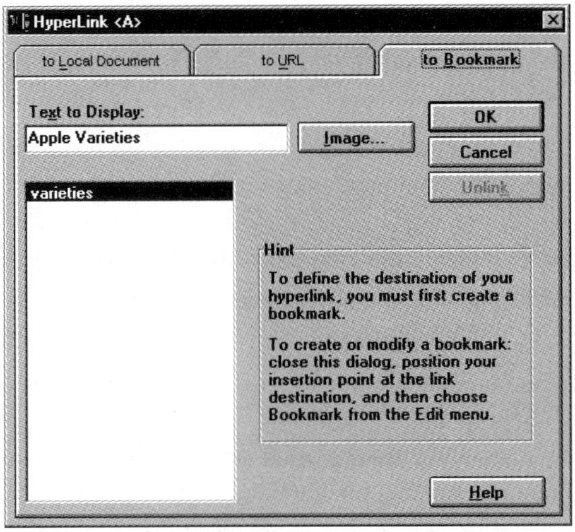

Figure 7.4 The HyperLink to Bookmark tab.

Anchor Links to Another Document

It's easy to create hyperlinks to bookmarks within the same document, but there's no simple command in Internet Assistant that will define an anchor link to another file. If you want to provide pointers to bookmarks in other documents, you'll have to go into the source code and modify the tag as follows:

1. Create a link to the local document or URL that contains the target bookmark.
2. Save the document as HyperText Markup Language (HTML).
3. Close the document.
4. Reopen the document with the Confirm Conversions option active. When the Convert File dialog box asks for a file type, choose Text Only.
5. Find the link you just created. For example, if the destination is the orchards.htm file, the source code of the link will look like this:

```
<A HREF="orchards.htm">grow your own</A>
```

6. To add a bookmark to the tag, insert the name of the bookmark (in this case, *varieties*) in this format:

```
<A HREF="orchards.htm#varieties">grow your own</A>
```

7. Save the document as Text Only.
8. Close the document and reopen it as HTML to continue editing it with Internet Assistant.

Links to Other Internet Resources

Other links

As you know, a URL may point to just about any kind of file on the Internet. Up until now, all the examples in this chapter have been HTML documents, but that's just one option. You can include links in your Web page to FTP directories or to a single file in a directory, to Gopher servers, or Usenet news groups. You can also create a URL that automates the process of sending an e-mail message to a designated recipient.

Therefore, if you want to point your readers to a nifty program or data file that's available in an anonymous FTP archive or a Gopher server someplace on the Internet, you can place a link to that file on your Web page. When a user clicks on the link, their browser will download a copy of the file or display the Gopher menu. Depending on the browser and the file type, the user might see the contents of the downloaded file in the browser itself or in some other file viewer, or store the file directly to disk.

Copying Links

Imitation is the sincerest form...

As you assemble your Web page, there's another way to add links to URLs. When you discover a Web page, FTP directory, or other resource that you want to link to, you can copy the URL and paste it directly into the page you're writing. This is a good technique to use when you're searching the World Wide Web for links because it guarantees that you get both the URL and the title of the destination page exactly right.

Here's the procedure:

1. If you are currently editing an HTML document, reduce the size of the document window.
2. Open a new document and switch to Web Browse view.
3. Use the Open URL command or links in other Web pages to jump to the URL you want to use as a link in your own document.
4. Open the Edit menu and select the Copy HyperLink command.

5. Return to Edit mode and go back to the HTML page that you are editing.
6. Place your cursor at the location where you want the link to appear.
7. Open the Edit menu and select the Paste command. The title of the URL will appear in your document as a link, with the correct URL in the HREF tag.

It's also possible to copy a link from your History list. As Figure 7.5 shows, there's a Copy HyperLink button in the History List dialog box. Don't try to use this method to create a relative link to a local file; the link won't work properly.

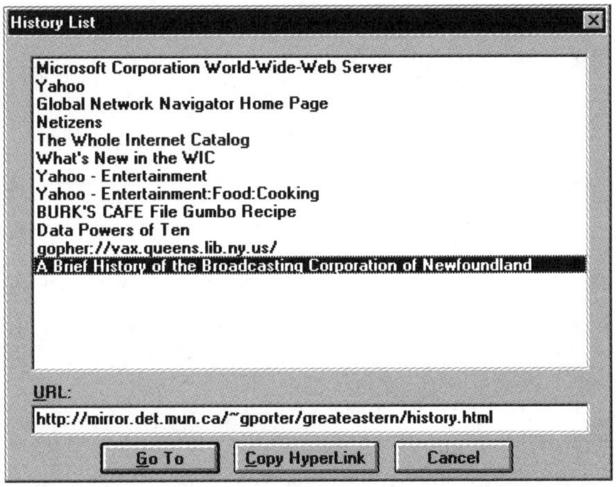

Figure 7.5 The History List.

ADDING GRAPHIC IMAGES TO YOUR DOCUMENT

> Look here, upon this picture, and on this.
>
> William Shakespeare
> *Hamlet*

A Web page with nothing but text may be full of great information, but it's going to look dull, gray, and boring compared to pages with colorful artwork integrated into the document. On the other hand, a Web page with no pictures will move across the Internet a lot faster, and you won't have to worry about how the page looks to people who use character-based browsers like Lynx. It's probably best to find a compromise, with no more than two or three medium-size pictures or five or six tiny ones per page.

Use small images.

Don't ever use huge pictures in a Web page. Enormous graphics are almost always a sign of a poorly designed Web site. They take forever to download, and many of your potential readers will give up and go away before the page is finished. As a rule of thumb, no single image file should be bigger than about 20K. Remember that the size of a graphics file increases with the area, which is equal to the height multiplied by the width. Therefore, if a 2×2-inch picture is a 19K file, a 6×4-inch version of the same image would require about 114K. In almost every case, the added size isn't worth the extra time needed to transfer the file.

If you're working with full-color pictures, you might also want to try reducing the number of colors in the image. Many graphics programs can perform this kind of conversion.

Image Formats

It's important to note that there are two quite different ways to handle graphic images. Inline images appear within Web pages as illustrations or decorations. Internet Assistant permits you to use inline images in either the .gif or JPEG (.jpg) formats, but .gif is the better choice because more browsers know how to recognize it.

The big picture

If it's important to provide a full-screen copy of a picture, it's a better idea to make that picture an external image rather than part (or all) of a Web page. **External images** are pictures that are not part of the HTML document, but that a reader downloads by clicking on a link, just like links to any other file type. Most browsers associate various file extensions with viewer programs that display those files after they've been downloaded. External images can use any graphic format, but it's a good idea to use the most common formats such as .gif or .tif.

Where to Find Images

Clip art

Placing a picture on the Internet, either as a downloadable file or as part of a Web page, is a form of publication, and therefore if you don't create your own images, you must either obtain permission to reproduce the image from the copyright owner, or use pictures that are in the public domain, such as those in clip art collections. You can download lots of clip art from online services like CompuServe and America Online, and from commercial collections of clip art and stock photographs. One good mail-order source is the Image Club catalog, which you can request by telephone (800-387-9193) or on the Internet (http://www.adobe.com/imageclub). Corel also publishes many collections of stock photos that you can find at many software retailers. If you have a good scanner, or if you can find a computer graphics service bureau, you can also create your own digital images from photographs or drawings. And, of course, you can use a graphics program like Corel Draw or Adobe Illustrator to create new online images.

Image conversion programs

If you have an image you want to use in your HTML document, but it's in the wrong format, you'll want to convert it to .gif. I've had good luck converting pictures with a commercial program called Hijaak and with a shareware product called PaintShop Pro, which you can find on all the online services or via anonymous FTP from the archive at ftp.cica.indiana.edu/pub/pc/win3. You can also use a conversion program to adjust the size of a picture to fit the layout of your page.

It's possible to insert an image located on another Web server directly into an HTML document, but it's a better idea to import a copy of the picture to your own computer and insert it into your Web page from there. Otherwise, you run the risk of losing control of an essential piece of your own layout.

When you include a picture in an HTML document, remember that the picture will appear on the page in full size; you can't use the tools in Word to change the dimensions as you can in other Word documents. Therefore, you'll have to use a graphics program to change the size before you import it. Smaller images are best, both because they take less time to transfer and because a wide image might not fit on a relatively small screen without horizontal scrolling.

Graphics as Illustrations

The big apple

I found the picture of a big red apple in Figure 7.6 on America Online. It loses some contrast in black and white, but it's really impressive in color.

I gave my love an apple...

Let's add it to the Apple Cider Home Page:

1. Move the .gif image to the same directory that contains your HTML document.

Figure 7.6 An image for the Apple Cider Home Page.

2. Place the cursor at the point in your page where you want to insert the picture. If you want the image in a new line (say, under a heading), place the cursor in a new paragraph.
3. Open the Insert menu and select the Picture command, or click the Picture button in the formatting toolbar.
4. When the dialog box in Figure 7.7 appears, find the name of file in the file selector.

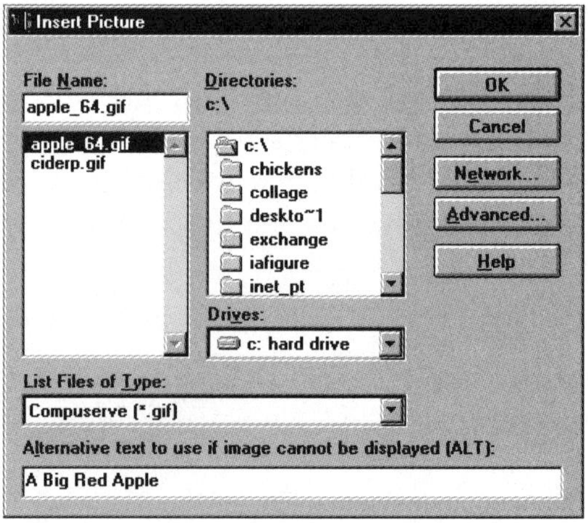

Figure 7.7 The Insert Picture dialog box.

5. Type a short description of the image in the Alternative Text field at the bottom on the dialog box. If a reader tries to visit your Web site with a browser that can't handle pictures, it will display the text in this field instead.
6. Click the Advanced button.
7. Choose one of the radio buttons in the Text Alignment (ALIGN) box. This won't have any effect in Internet Assistant, but many other browsers use this specification to set the exact location of the image relative to text in the same line.
8. Click the OK button to close the Advanced Options dialog and again to close the Insert Picture dialog box.

Figure 7.8 shows the Apple Cider Home Page with the apple picture inserted. Since the picture is in a separate line, the alignment doesn't make any difference.

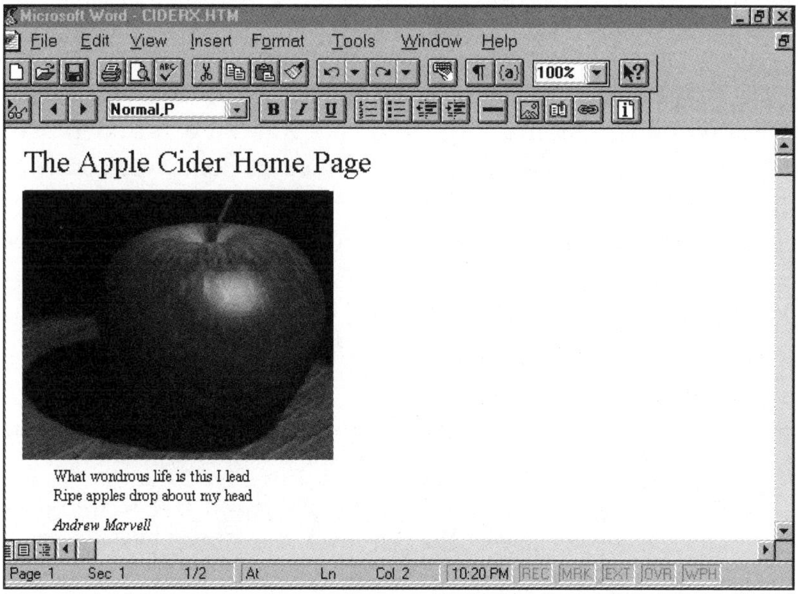

Figure 7.8 The Apple Cider Home Page with a picture added.

Show the flag.

You can also place an image within a line of text. Again, place the cursor at the exact location where you want the graphic and use the Insert Picture command. For example, in Figure 7.9, I've added little

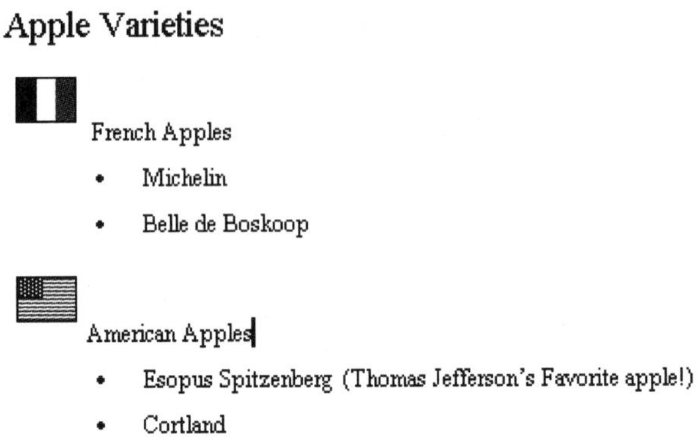

Figure 7.9 Images in line with text.

French and American flags to the list of apple types. In this sample, the pictures are at the left side of the line, but they could just as easily be between words.

Graphics as Design Elements

As I've explained, you can't completely control the appearance of text in a Web page because each browser may use different sizes and styles for various text elements. The differences may be subtle, but they're enough to frustrate an art director who wants complete control of the final product.

One partial solution to this problem is to create graphic images that incorporate both text and pictures. Programs like Corel Draw and Adobe Illustrator are ideal tools for this kind of work. If you're not up to drawing your own pictures, you can use a graphics program to combine text and clip art into a single image. For example, in Figure 7.10, I have combined a decorative typeface with a clip art picture of an old-fashioned apple cider press.

There are a couple of disadvantages to this approach. Images take a lot longer to transfer across the Internet than text; and users whose browsers can't handle graphics and those who have instructed their browsers to ignore graphic images won't see your artwork at all. But if you're willing to accept that compromise, using a moderate number of images to a page is probably the best possible way to add color and interesting design to your Web site.

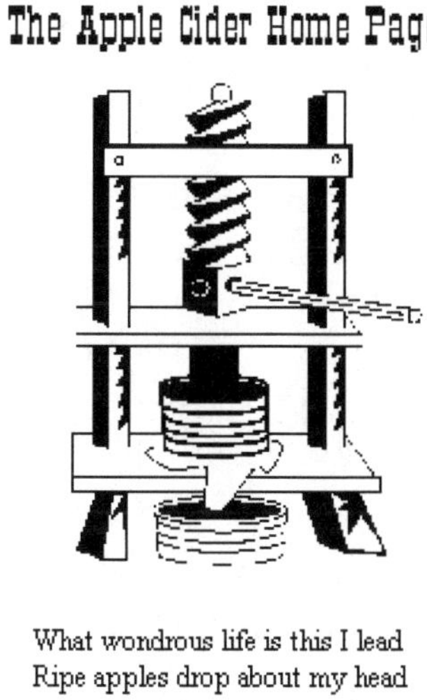

Figure 7.10 An image combined with decorative type.

Repeating Images

More of the same

Sometimes you may want to use the same small image in more than one location in the same Web page. For example, you might want to use your company logo at both the top and bottom of a long document, or even as a separator between sections. Many HTML designers also use a single icon for all the links in a home page.

When a browser sees a tag pointing to an image that it has already downloaded, it uses the version already in its memory, rather than repeating the download.

Graphics as Links

A graphic image can also be a link to a URL or a local file, just like a word or phrase. Here are some uses for images as links:

- A thumbnail-size version of a picture on your home page might be a link to a larger version of the same image.
- A logo or other symbol (such as a flag) might be a link to a Web page or other resource connected with the organization or company who uses that logo.

- A picture could be a link to a page with information about the subject of the picture. The destination link might have a bigger version of the same picture along with some text.
- A graphic image with the name of the link in a fancy typeface might replace or duplicate a text link.

As you play with the design of your Web pages, you will probably think of many other uses for graphic links.

Adding links to pictures

Creating a graphic link combines defining a link with inserting a picture:

1. Move your cursor to the location where you want the graphic link to appear in your Web page. The link may be a separate paragraph or within a line of text.
2. Open the Insert menu and choose the HyperLink command, or click the HyperLink button in the formatting toolbar.
3. When the HyperLink <A> dialog box appears, choose the tab that describes the location of the local file, bookmark, or URL that is the link's destination. The top part of all three tabs looks like Figure 7.11.

Figure 7.11 Click the Image button to insert a graphic link.

4. Click the Image button. The same Insert Picture dialog box that you use to place a nonlinking picture in a Web page will appear.
5. Use the file selector to select the .gif file that contains the picture you want to insert. Click the OK button to return to the HyperLink dialog box. Remember to type a short description of the link in the Alternative text field for browsers that don't accept graphics.
6. Specify the destination of the link in the lower part of the dialog box just as you did for a text link.
7. Click the OK button to insert the picture and create the link. Notice that the newly inserted picture has a blue border around it to identify it as a link.

Location-Sensitive Image Maps

As you explore the World Wide Web, you will discover Web pages with maps, graphic menus, and other images with more than one link within the same picture. Many of the classiest Web sites use these fancy "clickable images."

In order to create an image map, you need a separate map file that identifies regions within the image and assigns a destination to each region. To make it even more complicated, the exact format of the map file is different for different kinds of HTTP (HyperText Transfer Protocol) servers. In other words, if you're starting with Internet Assistant, you *can* get there from here, but you need a bunch of extra tools.

Map files

So the first thing to do is to talk to your system administrator or Internet service provider and ask for help creating a map file and a gateway script that will work with the type of server that will contain your Web site. That's not particularly satisfying to a dedicated do-it-yourselfer, but there you are.

Once you have the image file (the .gif file with the picture) and the map file, the rest is easy:

1. Place the cursor in the position where you want the image map to appear on your Web page.
2. Use the Insert HyperLink command to open the HyperLink <A> dialog box.
3. Choose the tab that identifies the location of the map file—either Local (on the same system as the HTML document) or URL (someplace else on the Internet).
4. Click the Image button to open the Insert Picture dialog box.
5. Choose the name and location of the image file.
6. Click the Advanced button.
7. Click on the Sensitive Map option to place a checkmark in the box. (See Figure 7.12.)
8. Click the OK button.
9. Type the URL or local name and path of the map file.
10. Click the OK button.

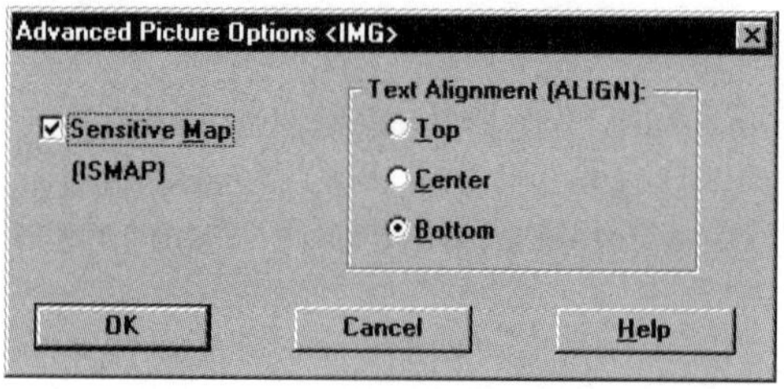

Figure 7.12 Click on the Sensitive Map option.

Quite honestly, you probably can't create an image map unless you can get help from somebody who knows how your particular server works with map files. Because it's not always the same, Internet Assistant doesn't create these things, and Microsoft doesn't give you enough information to build them on your own. So, in most cases, the best advice I can offer is this: Don't mess with image maps without advice and assistance from somebody who's done it before, preferably on the same HTTP server.

8 Creating HTML Documents: Forms and CGI Scripts

The shortest and best way to make your fortune is to let people see clearly that it is in their interests to promote yours.

Jean de La Bruyère
"Of the Gifts of Fortune," *Characters,* 1688

Up until now, I've been talking about just one kind of interactivity in a Web page: a reader clicks on a link and the browser jumps to another Unform Resource Locator (URL) or another location in the current Web page. You can also build other interactive tools into your documents. A link to a program script on a server can extract information from a database, operate a peripheral device such as a video camera, or perform any other task you can program a computer to do.

Forms follow function.

In addition, you can use a Web page to collect data from your readers through fill-in-the-blanks text fields, checkboxes, or menus that send commands or information requests from the browser to the Web server.

Writing scripts for the server is another story. In fact, it's another book. You can't use Internet Assistant to write a script. Some HTML editors include CGI scripting tools, but Internet Assistant is not among them. Separate server packages with scripting are available, but some of them are quite expensive—$2000 and up.

Before you can even think about writing a script, you need to know the operating system the server is using—UNIX? Windows NT? Something less common?—and the particular type of server program and scripting language that that operating system requires. UNIX and some other platforms may use the Common Gateway Interface or something similar to CGI, but you can't just write a generic script and automatically assume that it will work on your own service provider's server. If you're working with a server that doesn't use UNIX, you may have to use a completely different scripting language. Therefore, before you start, you must obtain specific instructions for the server you want to use. And, since a CGI script typically runs one or more programs on the server, the people in charge of maintaining the server will have something to say about the things you're allowing outsiders (your readers) to do on their computer.

Yet another call for help

You can see where this is leading. If you want to use any kind of interactive commands in your Web pages, you'll have to spend a lot of time talking to the system administrator for the server. And you'll either need to learn something about writing the actual scripts and programs yourself, or find somebody else to do it for you. If you think this all sounds similar to the way HTML handles image maps, you're right. Map files are a specialized variety of CGI script.

LINKS TO CGI SCRIPTS

> There is one outstandingly important fact regarding Spaceship Earth, and that is that no instruction book came with it.
>
> R. Buckminster Fuller
> *Operating Manual for Spaceship Earth*, 1969

Here's what happens when a reader clicks on a link to a CGI script:

1. The browser sends the link request to the server. Like every other link, it's a URL that identifies a specific file.
2. The server recognizes that the file named in the URL is a script, which it proceeds to carry out. The script may contain instructions to obtain information from a database, operate a piece of peripheral equipment (such as a video camera), or run yet another program which returns data to the script.
3. If necessary, the script converts the data to a format that the Web server can return to the browser as a file or an HTML document.
4. The browser receives and displays the data from the server.

Links to CGI scripts

From the browser's point of view, a script is just one more type of URL. You don't have to add anything special to your HTML document except the link to a script file because all the real action is happening on the server. Therefore, you can use Internet Assistant's formatting tools to add a link to a CGI script, just as you would add any other link:

1. Select the text you want to use as the link, or the location where you want to insert a linked image.
2. Select the Insert HyperLink command from either the Insert menu or the formatting toolbar.
3. Choose the To URL tab in the HyperLink <A> dialog box.
4. If the link is an image, click the Image button and select the image file from the Insert Picture dialog box.
5. Type the URL of the CGI script in the URL field.

That's pretty simple, but remember that you've only done half the job. Before the link to a script file will accomplish anything, you must also write the script program, install it on the server, and confirm that everything works properly. And, as I've already said, Internet Assistant can't help you with that.

FORMS

> Take thy beak from out my heart, and take thy form from off my door!
>
> Edgar Allan Poe
> "The Raven," 1845

Forms in HTML documents are an alternative to conventional links as a method for sending commands and data from a browser to a CGI script on a server. Forms can appear in a Web page in several…um… forms:

- Fill-in-the-blanks text fields
- Pushbuttons that send specific commands to the browser
- Checkboxes
- Radio buttons
- Drop-down menus with two or more options

The real work is on the server.

When a visitor to your Web site uses a form, the visitor's browser sends a command or a block of data to a specified destination. Therefore, you can use forms to request information from a reader, such as a name and address or a password, or let the reader select items from a list to request information or to submit answers to a poll. If and when secure data transmission over the Internet becomes practical, you could also request a credit card number or other account information, either to accept an order for goods or services, or to charge your would-be readers for access to the "good stuff" on your Web site.

Before you jump into forms design with both feet, you need to be aware of a couple of important issues. First, the server that contains a Web page that includes forms must have software that receives and processes the information that readers submit. Therefore, you must carefully coordinate your activities with the system administrator or Internet service provider who operates the server. If you plan to use forms, remember to ask about them when you arrange to place your HTML documents on a server. Fortunately, if your server can handle forms at all, there's a standard method for handling them, so you don't have the same kind of compatibility problem that occurs with image maps. Assuming your system administrator or service provider has told you their server can handle forms, you can go ahead and include them in your document, but you'll have to arrange to do something with the information that comes back from your readers.

Second, before you add forms to your site, you should remember that early versions of many Web browsers did not support forms, so people using those browsers won't be able to send information back to you. This is less of a problem than it used to be, but it can still be a source of irritation for some users.

Almost everything you know is wrong.

At a guess, at least three-quarters of all Word users have never done anything with forms in conventional Word documents. Therefore, I'm assuming that most people reading this don't have a working knowledge of the Forms dialog boxes. If I'm mistaken, bear with me; even if you think you understand forms in Word, much of it is wrong when it comes to HTML.

Microsoft has tried to use the existing Forms dialog boxes in Word to create HTML forms, but it's a clumsy fit. This is very much like using a kitchen knife as a screwdriver—you can make it work, but that's not what it was designed for. Many fields in the dialog boxes have no function in HTML, and others have names that no longer relate to their functions. The whole process would probably have worked better if they had started over from scratch and created new dialogs, but since they didn't, there's a lot of room for confusion. Keep reminding yourself: "This is free software. It's worth every penny I paid for it."

Forms begin with a <FORM> tag and end with a </FORM> tag. HTML Edit View displays these tags as "Top of Form" and "Bottom of Form" boundaries, as shown in Figure 8.1. The Top of Form and Bottom of Form boundaries will not be visible when you save the document and open it in a browser.

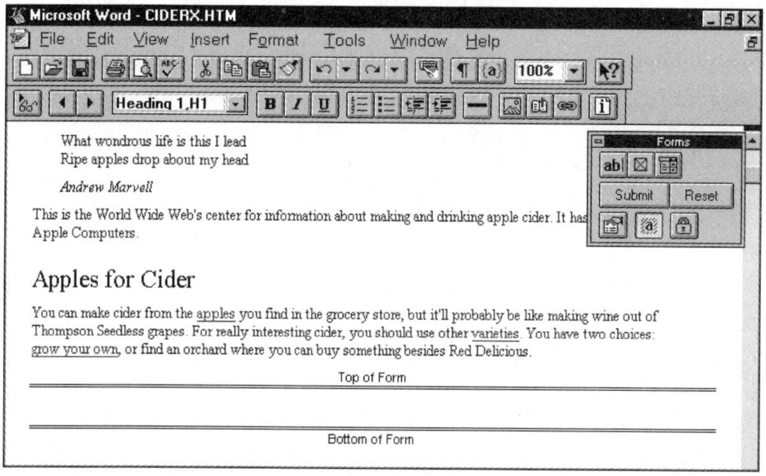

Figure 8.1 The Top and Bottom of Form boundaries.

All of the form fields between Top of Form and Bottom of Form (or more accurately, between <FORM> and </FORM>) are part of a single form. You can have as many forms in a document as you want, as long as each form has a pair of boundaries and a Submit button.

Here's what you have to do to place forms in your document:

1. Place the cursor in the location where you want the form to appear.
2. Open the Insert menu and select the Form Field command.
3. When the New Form message box appears, click the Continue button.

4. When the Form Field dialog box appears, click the Cancel button. (You don't want to use it because you can do everything from the toolbar instead.)
5. Move the cursor between the Top of Form and Bottom of Form boundaries and type the text that you want to appear to the left of the first form field.
6. Choose the type of form field you want to add from the Forms toolbar and click the button to insert it at the cursor.
7. Click the Form Field Options button to configure the field.
8. Add additional text and form fields as necessary.

The Forms toolbox

If you drag the Forms toolbox to the top, bottom, or either side of the Word window, it will change to a toolbar. Figure 8.2 shows the Forms toolbox.

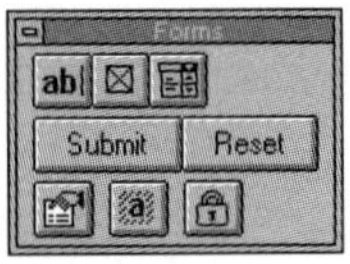

Figure 8.2 The Forms toolbox.

The Forms toolbar/toolbox has five buttons that specify the type of form field you're inserting. Three of the form fields are similar to the ones you've seen in Windows dialog boxes.

While you're working on a form field, you might want to click the Shading button to make the fields easier to see. Shading won't be visible when you save the document and open it in a browser.

Text Entry Forms

Your name here

A **text form field** is a blank space where a reader can type text, numbers, symbols, or spaces. Text form fields may provide space for either a single line for an answer to a simple question (such as the reader's name or password) or a larger area for extended comments.

The HTML tag for a single line is <INPUT TYPE="TEXT">. To create a single-line text field, follow these steps:

1. Place the cursor where you want to text field to appear, within the Form boundaries.
2. Click the Text Form Field button in the Forms toolbar to insert a new form field at the cursor.
3. Double-click on the form field you just created. The Text Form Field Options dialog box in Figure 8.3 appears. This is the same dialog box that Word uses for other forms, and some of the fields in the dialog box are not used in Internet Assistant.

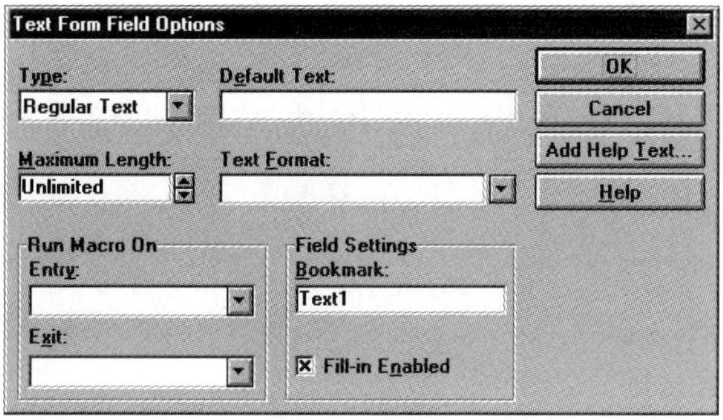

Figure 8.3 The Text Form Field Options dialog box.

4. The default length of the text form field is five characters. To allow the form to accept more than five characters, select the text in the Maximum Length field, delete it, and then type the maximum number of characters you want to allow, up to a maximum of 80. To allow for unexpectedly long names, it's a good idea to allow more characters than you absolutely need.
5. When the browser returns the information in this field to the server, you might want to send a brief description along with the data the user types into the field. This label won't appear in your Web page, but it may help you later when you try to make sense of the data your readers have sent back to the server. To define a field label, click the Add Help Text button and select the Help Key (F1) tab to display the Help Text dialog box in Figure 8.4.
6. If you want a default text to appear in the form field (you probably don't), type the text in the Default Text field.

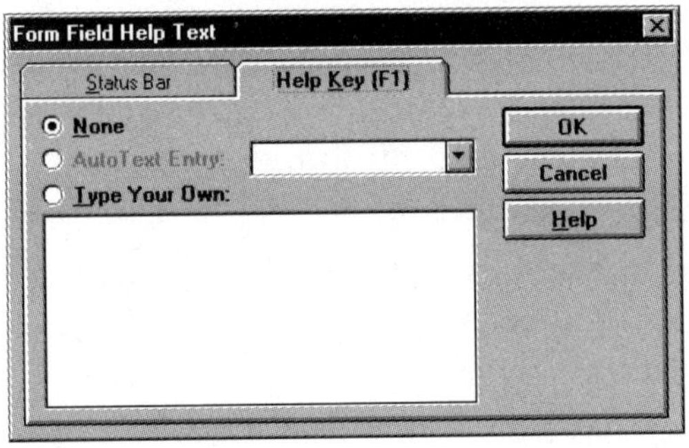

Figure 8.4 Type the description in the Type Your Own field.

Big text fields

The HTML tag for a text field with more than one line is <TEXTAREA>. Internet Assistant uses the same dialog box to specify large text areas as it does for single-line text fields. Follow these steps to create an extended text field:

1. Place the cursor where you want to text field to appear, between the Form boundaries.
2. Click the Text Form Field button in the Forms toolbar to insert a new form field at the cursor.
3. Double-click on the new form field. The Form Field Options dialog box appears.
4. Click the Add Help Text button. When the Form Field Help Text dialog box appears, choose the Status Bar tab.
5. To set the size of the text form field, click on the Type Your Own radio button and use this format in the box:

   ```
   ROWS="x"
   COLS="y"
   ```

   In place of *x*, type the height of the text area, in rows. In place of *y*, type the width, in columns.
6. To specify a name for the data the browser returns to the server from this field, click on the Help Key (F1) tab, choose the Type Your Own radio button, and type the description in the box.

Check Box Forms

Check and double-check

A **check box** usually appears in a browser as an empty square. When a user clicks on the box, an X or checkmark appears or disappears. In most cases, check boxes are used for lists of options where the reader can select more than one option at the same time. To add a check box form field:

1. Place the cursor in the location where you want the check box, within the Forms boundaries.
2. Click the Check Box button in the Forms toolbar.
3. Double-click on the new form field to open the Check Box Form Field Options dialog box in Figure 8.5.

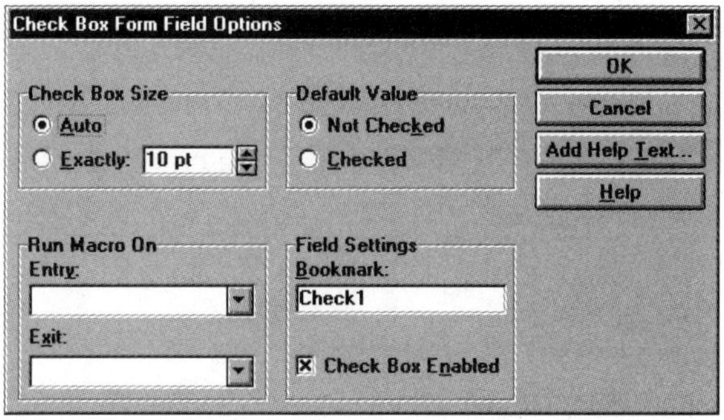

Figure 8.5 The Check Box Form Field Options dialog box.

4. The Default Value box in the Check Box Form Field Options dialog box specifies whether or not this check box will appear with a check in it when a browser downloads this document. In most cases, you will want the default to be Not Checked.
5. Click the Add Help Text button and choose the Help Key (F1) tab.
6. Choose the Type Your Own radio button and type a description of this form field in the box. The description must be identical for all of the check box fields in a list. The browser uses this description to identify this set of options to the server. None of the other fields in the Check Box Form Field Options dialog box apply to HTML documents.

7. Repeat the procedure for each additional check box you want to add to the document.

Radio Buttons

Multiple choices

Like the buttons on your car radio, radio buttons are single-choice options. When a user selects one radio button from a list, the previously selected option is automatically unselected. In Internet Assistant, a set of radio buttons looks just like a list of check boxes, but in Netscape and other browsers, radio buttons are round instead of square, like the radio buttons in Windows dialog boxes.

This is the procedure for creating a set of radio buttons:

1. Move your cursor to the location where you want the first button to appear, within the Forms boundaries.
2. Type the text that you want next to the first radio button.
3. Click the Check Box Form Field button in the Forms toolbar to place a check box in the document at the cursor's current position.
4. Double-click on the check box you just created. The Check Box Form Field Options dialog box opens.
5. The Bookmark field in the Field Settings box currently says "Check1." To convert this check box to a radio button, change it to **Check1_RD.**
6. Click the Add Help Text button and choose the Help Key (F1) tab.
7. Select the Type Your Own option and type a brief description of this set of radio buttons in the box.
8. Now select the Status Bar tab and choose the Type Your Own option.
9. In the Type Your Own box, type a brief description of this radio button, using this format: **VALUE="*description*"**. The *description* must be different for each radio button.
10. Repeat the process for each additional radio button you want in the same set of options. For each option, increase the number in the Bookmark field: **Check2_RD, Check3_RD,** and so forth.

When a reader selects a radio button, the browser sends the server both the name that is common to the set of options and the specific description of the option that was selected.

Drop-Down Menus

One from column A; two from column B

Drop-down forms are like drop-down menus in Windows; a reader can select an option from a menu. Some browsers allow a user to select more than one option, but Internet Assistant doesn't support the MULTIPLE attribute. I'll tell you how to add it later in this section.

To create a drop-down form field:

1. Place your cursor in the location where you want the form field to appear, within the Form boundaries.
2. Click the Drop-Down Form Field button in the Forms toolbar.
3. Double-click on the new form to open the Options dialog box in Figure 8.6.

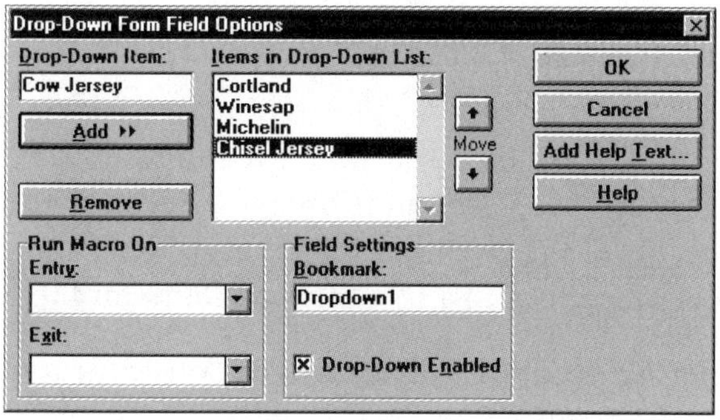

Figure 8.6 The Drop-Down Form Field Options dialog box.

4. Type the first item you want to include in the drop-down list in the Drop-Down Item field and click the Add button. Repeat the process for each additional item you want in the same menu. Internet Assistant accepts a maximum of 25 items in a single list, which is probably too many for a reader to conveniently use.
5. To delete an item from the menu, select it and click the Remove button. To change the order, select an item in the list and use the Move arrow buttons.

6. Click the Add Help Text button and choose the Help Key (F1) tab.
7. Choose the Type Your Own radio button and type a description of the list in the box. The browser returns this description to the server along with the option the reader has selected.
8. Click the OK buttons to close the dialog boxes.
9. Click the Protect Form button in the Forms toolbar to display the new drop-down form.

The Submit Button

You will submit to my wishes.

To understand why a form needs a Submit command, let's review exactly what happens in **HyperText Transfer Protocol**, the system that moves HTML documents around the Internet. When you enter a URL into a browser, the browser finds the file named in the URL, transfers a copy to your computer, and displays it. It's important to remember that a browser performs a *download*, rather than setting up a live connection to the source of the URL.

Therefore, when you fill in a text field form or select an option from a check box, radio button, or drop-down menu, you're really storing your entries on your own computer. The server doesn't know what you've done until you upload it. That's where the Submit command button comes in. When a user enters the Submit command, the browser sends the contents of the form fields to the server.

Follow this procedure to add a Submit command to a form:

1. Place the cursor in the location where you want the Submit command button to appear.
2. Click the Submit button in the Forms toolbar. The Form Submit Button dialog box in Figure 8.7 appears.
3. The command button can contain either text or a graphic image. For text, choose the Text option and type the text you want inside the button into the text box. For an image, choose the Custom Button option, click the Select Picture button and use the file selector to specify the image.
4. The Submission Information box in the Form Submit Button dialog box controls the way your HTML document returns data to the

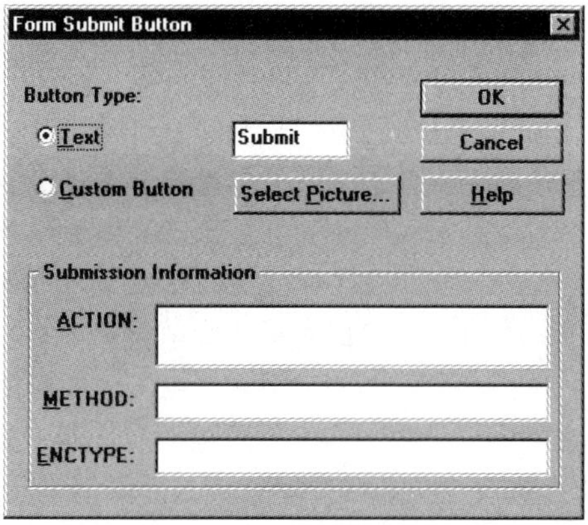

Figure 8.7 The Form Submit Button dialog box.

server. In the ACTION field, type the URL of the script on the server to which you want to send the data from this form. You'll have to obtain the URL from the server's system administrator.

5. You can choose to submit data from a form to a CGI script in two ways: POST and GET. POST sends the data without variables or arguments. GET sends coded data as part of the URL that the browser sends back to the CGI script on the server, which converts the coded URL back to useful data. If the URL in the ACTION field begins with http://, the METHOD should be POST. For any other type of URL, the METHOD should be GET. GET is the default.

   GET submissions can become very long if the form has a lot of options in it. In fact, a GET URL can sometimes have more characters than the server can accept. POST doesn't have this problem. If at all possible, arrange with the administrator of the server to use an CGI script with an http:// URL so that POST is the appropriate submission method.

6. The ENCTYPE (Encoding Type) field specifies the format that a POST submission uses for the form data that it sends to the CGI script on the server. The default is **application/x-www-form-urlencoded**, but you'll have to obtain the correct format for your script from the administrator of the server.

The Reset Button

Reset A RESET command in a form clears all of the fields in the form and returns them to the default values. It's a courtesy to your readers to include a Reset button in your forms so they can change their entries before submitting them. Reset does not send any data back to the server.

To add a Reset button to a form, place the cursor in the location where you want the button to appear and click the Reset button in the Forms toolbar.

Putting It All Together

Now that I've described each type of form field you can use in an HTML document, let's create a Web page with forms. As an example, I've created a sign-up page for the Western Washington Tree Fruit Foundation.

You can place your forms on separate pages or make them part of a page that also contains other information and conventional hypertext links. It would be possible to make the entire page into a form, but it's generally a good idea to include a heading and some text at the top of the page, just in case somebody links directly to the page, without the context that your own home page supplies. Therefore, you should first create a main heading and a few lines of text that explain what the page is about.

To add a form to the page, place the cursor at the location where you want to place the form, open the Insert menu, and select the Form Field command. After you close the Options dialog box, the screen looks like Figure 8.8, with the cursor visible between the Form boundaries and the Forms toolbar.

Within the Form boundaries, use the buttons in the Forms toolbar to insert and configure individual form fields. Figure 8.9 shows an assortment of text field forms, check boxes, and drop-down menus.

The fields are gray in Word because the Form Field Shading button is active. In most browsers, the text fields will be inside boxes. All text form fields are five characters wide in Edit View, regardless of the actual configuration.

Finally, every form needs a Submit command, so we'll add it from the Forms toolbar. Rather than the default "Submit" button, we'll create one that says, "Join WWTFF." When you save this form and open it up in a browser, it will look like Figure 8.10.

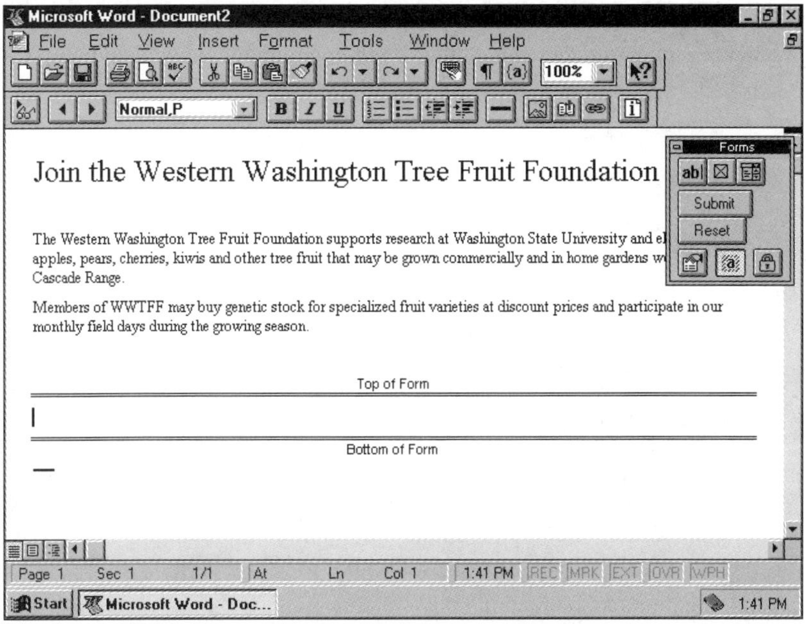

Figure 8.8 An empty form in an HTML document.

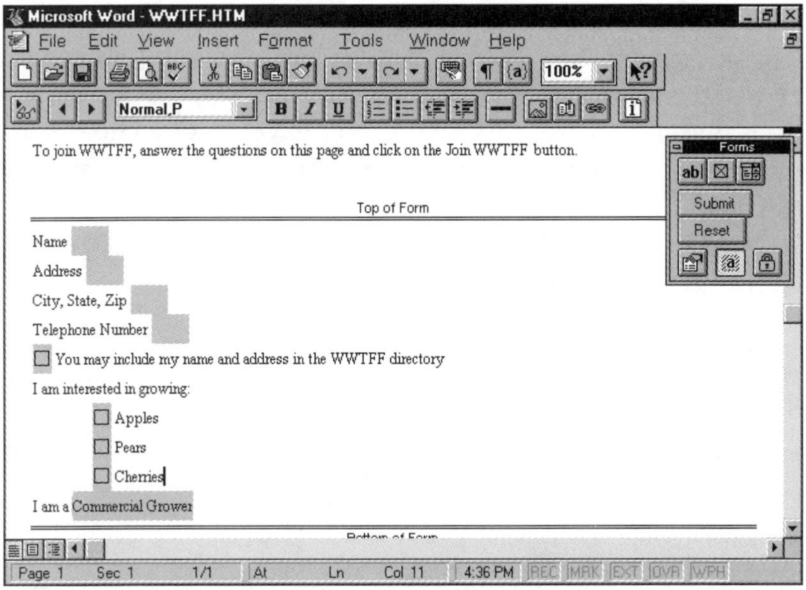

Figure 8.9 Form fields in Internet Assistant Edit View.

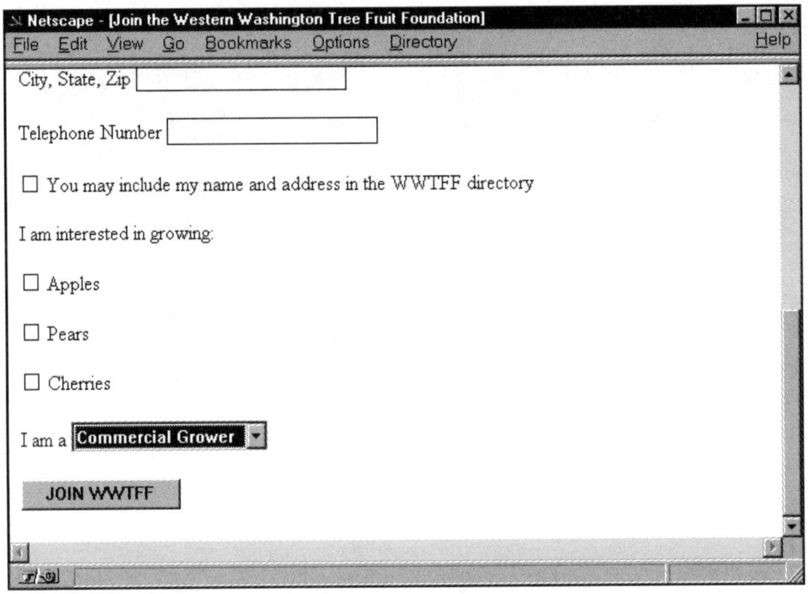

Figure 8.10 The same form in Netscape.

Bribes are always welcome.

Adding forms to an HTML document in Word and Internet Assistant is not much more complicated than adding any other kind of text or graphic element, but a form won't do you any good unless you've also created a CGI script on your server. And, since that's more than you can do with Internet Assistant, you have several choices: forget about forms, find Web server software that supports script writing, or ask for help from the people who run your server. If you choose the ask-for-help route, I've found that a batch of chocolate chip cookies or a jug of freshly pressed apple cider can do wonders.

9 What Can You Do with HTML Pages?

We are so presumptuous that we should like to be known all over the world, even by people who will only come when we are no more. Such is our vanity that the good opinion of half a dozen of the people around us gives us pleasure and satisfaction.

Blaise Pascal
Pensées, 1670

You've created an HTML document. Now what?

Servers

Before anybody else can see what you've done, you'll have to put the document on a server. A Web server stores HTML documents and other files and sends copies of those files when it receives requests from a Web browser such as Netscape, Mosaic, or the browser in Internet Assistant. The server also handles CGI gateway scripts and processes data from image maps and HTML forms. You don't need a server to write your Web pages (you've got Internet Assistant for that), but you'll need one to make them available to other people through the Internet or a local network. In most cases, the server is a dedicated computer with a permanent, high-speed connection to the Internet, rather than a general-purpose desktop machine.

In this chapter, we'll talk about finding an Internet Web server, and about other things you can do with HTML—creating a private Web on a local area network (LAN) and distributing HTML documents on diskette or CD-ROM as interactive text files.

PUTTING YOUR PAGES ON THE INTERNET

> The important thing about the so-called "communications industry" is that it is basically concerned with merchandising. News is a kind of by-product and if you want to sell things, you don't want to offend anybody.
>
> I. F. Stone
> *The Listener* magazine, 1963

Setting up and running your own server is possible, but it requires a lot of time and money. In most cases, a server runs on a dedicated computer; server software is available for UNIX, Windows NT, and most other operating systems, including DOS and Windows. However, the hardware and software are just the beginning. You'll also need a permanent link to the Internet with enough capacity to handle the demand for access to your site (it's not uncommon to experience several thousand "hits" a day, so a 28.8 kbps telephone line is not adequate). Then you have to think about learning to write CGI scripts and image map programs, or hiring somebody to write them for you.

Serious money

Depending on the computer, the network hardware, the high-speed link, and the server software you choose, it could easily cost $5000 or more to get started and another couple of hundred dollars a month for your Internet connection. That's a lot of money to put up a Web page with pictures of your daughter and her favorite brownie recipe.

Fortunately, there are some other ways to make your Web site accessible to the Internet. It's almost always easier and less expensive to place your Web site on an existing server. Once a server is up and running, the only thing needed to support more Web pages on that server is space on a disk.

Find an existing server.

The first place to look for a Web server is your own Internet service provider. If you're connected to the Internet through a university or a large corporation, there may already be a place to put Web pages on your LAN or campus-wide network. There's probably a network administrator who can answer most of your questions. Many commercial Internet access services also offer Web space to their customers, either as part of the access package or for an additional monthly charge; if they didn't mention it when you signed up, ask the customer support center if they can help.

Internet Presence Providers

If your own access provider can't give you space on a server, don't despair. There's a booming category of businesses called **Internet presence providers** who offer space on their Web servers in exchange for a monthly fee. As I write this, the local NPR station is broadcasting a commercial for a "Web page development specialist" who is anxious to put my business on the Internet. Half a dozen others have advertisements in the Sunday newspaper. The Yahoo directory lists almost two thousand presence providers at http://www.yahoo.com/Business_and_Economy/Companies/Internet_Presence_Providers. Some of these folks charge as little as $15 a month for space on a disk, whereas others want $150 an hour for design and development time, plus $100 or more per month to maintain your Web site.

Value for your money

Like most things in life, you get what you pay for. If you have a simple Web site with nothing but text, images, and few links to other URLs, you really don't need much more than space on a disk; if your documents include image maps and interactive forms, you'll have to find a presence provider who can help you prepare and maintain a CGI script.

You can transfer your Web pages from your own PC to a server through the Internet, so the server can be physically located almost anywhere. However, there's a real advantage to choosing a nearby server if you're planning a Web site that uses forms and image maps because you'll probably have to work closely with the people who develop and maintain your CGI scripts for you.

The following sections describe some other factors to consider as you evaluate a potential home for your Web site.

Full-Time Access

24 hours a day

Your Web site should be on line 24 hours a day, seven days a week. Some small amount of downtime for maintenance is acceptable, but you shouldn't even consider putting your pages on a server that limits access to specified hours or days.

Large Capacity

Adequate power

The computer where the server software is running should have adequate processing power, and the link to the Internet backbone should have enough bandwidth to handle many simultaneous access requests from Web browsers. Even if your own Web pages attract only a few visitors, your Web site could suffer from slow data transfer if you're sharing the server with an archive of *Playboy* centerfolds that receives 30,000 download requests every day. Since you can't predict or control the content of somebody else's Web site, you should make sure the server can handle a significant load.

Script Support

CGI scripts

Clickable pictures, interactive forms, and other advanced features can make the difference between an ordinary Web site and one that stands out among the millions (yes, millions) of others to deliver an effective message. As Chapter 8 explained, you can use Internet Assistant to create a page that includes links to scripts, but you need other tools and programming knowledge to run the scripts themselves on a server. Your Internet presence provider should be able to work with you to develop scripts that meet the specific requirements of your Web pages.

Custom Domain Name

Memorable URL

It's not absolutely necessary, but if you're planning to encourage people to visit your Web site, you might want to create an easy-to-remember URL for your home page. An address like http://www.carol.com is a lot more memorable than http://provider.com/users/carol/web/index.html. Your network administrator or presence provider should be able to create an alias that points directly to your home page. You'll almost certainly have to pay an extra fee to register your domain name with the service that maintains the world-wide domain name service database.

Security

Protected pages

You may hope that everybody in the world will visit your Web site, but you don't want anybody to make changes to the content of your pages without your knowledge or permission. Your own account should be the only one with write access to your files.

Cost

Best value

If you spend some time comparing similar services from more than one supplier, you'll probably discover a wide range of prices. The least expensive isn't always the best choice, but there's no good reason to spend two or three times as much as you really have to.

Maintaining Your Own Server

Do it yourself?

It may make sense to place your Web site on your own server if you have a spare computer, direct access to a LAN with a high-speed connection to the Internet, and the technical knowledge and experience to maintain them.

You'll also have to install server software and learn how to use it. Two excellent sources of information about setting up servers and writing CGI scripts are *Teach Yourself Web Publishing with HTML in a Week,* and *Teach Yourself More Web Publishing with HTML,* both by Laura Lemay (both published by Sams in 1995). To find online information about servers, go to the Yahoo directory (http://www/yahoo.com) and look at the Computers and Internet:Internet:World Wide Web: HTTP:Servers page.

Simple Servers for Simple Web Pages

Use a file server.

By now, you may be ready to decide that finding a Web server may be more trouble than it's worth—but if none of your Web pages uses forms, image maps, or links to other CGI scripts, there's another, simpler approach. You can place your HTML documents and graphic image files on a computer that supports just about any other kind of Internet file server, including FTP and Gopher servers. Web browsers don't care where they obtain HTML files because they download the files to the local computer before they read them. Therefore, you don't always need a specialized Web server.

This opens up several options. Even if your Internet access provider doesn't have a Web server, they may include space on an FTP or Gopher server with SLIP, PPP, or UNIX shell accounts. Your service provider's customer support department can tell you if they have a file server and where to find it.

If you're connected to the Internet through a LAN, you can install an FTP server program on a PC. There are FTP servers in many TCP/IP connectivity packages, including the ones sold by IBM, NetManage, FTP Software, and WRQ/Reflection. Your LAN administrator may already have one of these packages; if not, they're advertised in magazines like *Network World, Communications Week,* and *Data Communications*.

This technique has one important negative feature. Your Web site's URL is determined by the type of server it lives on; therefore, a Web site located on an FTP server will have a URL that begins with ftp://, rather than http://. This is going to confuse people who use the wrong URL to look for your pages.

Moving Your Files to the Server

One way or another, you've identified a server for your Web site. It might be on one of your own computers, or you may have made some kind of arrangement to use an existing server. The next step is to copy your HTML documents and graphics file to the server from the PC where you created them.

Relative links remain relative.

This is where the time and care you've taken to use relative links between documents and images, and between the individual pages in your Web site make your life easier. As long as you maintain the same relative file structure, all of your links should continue to work properly. In most cases, the easiest method is to keep all of your files in the same directory.

The specific procedure may be slightly different for different servers, but here are the steps you must complete:

1. Create a subdirectory on the server for your Web site.
2. Copy the files from your PC to the server. You can use FTP, or set up a telnet connection with a communications program such as Procomm or Crosstalk and use ZModem or some other file transfer protocol. If you use FTP, remember to transfer HTML documents as text files, and graphic images as binary files.
3. If you're using a UNIX server, change the file extensions of your .htm files to .html. If you're using some other operating system, ask your system administrator if you need to change file extensions.

4. Change the filename of your home page to index.html (or index.htm, as appropriate). This is the default filename that your server will upload if a browser does not request a specific document by name. For example, if the full URL of your home page is http://www.cider.com/index.html, the default URL for your Web site—http://www.cider.com—would also retrieve the home page file.

Identify your URL.

Once you have installed your Web site on a server, you should make a note of the home page's URL so you can tell other people about it. If somebody else maintains the server that contains your Web site, that person should be able to tell you its URL. If you've created your own server, you'll have to construct the URL out of the type of server (http, ftp, or whatever), the Domain Name System (DNS) address of the server, and the path to the directory that contains your home page. For example, if you're using a Web server with the DNS address www.cider.com and the home page HTML file is in the root directory, your Web site's URL would be http://www.cider.com. If the home page file is in a subdirectory called apple.cider (remember, this is UNIX), the URL would be http://www.cider.com/apple.cider.

TESTING YOUR WEB PAGES

> If at first you don't succeed, try again. Then quit: no use being a damn fool about it.
>
> W. C. Fields

The final step before you're ready to tell the world about your shiny new Web site is to test it. Make sure the text says what you want it to say, and check for spelling errors. Confirm that the hypertext links all work and that the graphic images are all in place.

Test and test some more.

Test it from your own Internet account, and test it from somebody else's account through a different service provider. Test it from a Macintosh, and test it from the computer at your local public library. Test it in color, and test it on a monochrome monitor. Test it with Internet Assistant, and test it with Netscape, Mosaic, and every other browser you can find. Test it through America Online, and test it through Microsoft Network. Test, test, test!

You get the idea. As you test, make sure your Web pages look good and make sense on as many systems and browsers as you can find. Each one will display your pages slightly (or more than slightly) differently. You'll be amazed to discover how the same document can look through more than one browser or platform.

After the first round of testing, fix whatever doesn't work the way you expected and test again. Keep testing until everything works properly.

PUBLICIZING YOUR WEB SITE

> The more you are talked about, the more you will wish to be talked about. The condemned murderer who is allowed to see the account of his trial in the Press is indignant if he finds a newspaper which has reported it inadequately. And the more he finds about himself in other newspapers, the more indignant he will be with the one whose reports are meagre. Politicians and literary men are in the same case.
>
> Bertrand Russell
> *Human Society in Ethics and Politics*, 1954

Hire a brass band.

Just because your Web site is in place, you won't have any visitors until you let people know that it exists. If you have a fat publicity budget, you can put up some billboards or hire one of those airplanes dragging a big banner with the URL of your home page in giant letters. If that's not practical, or if you want to reach people who actually use the World Wide Web, there are other, more focused techniques.

Look around the Web for other pages that contain information about the same or related topics. Send e-mail messages to the webmasters at those sites, tell them about your site (remember to include the URL), offer to add a link to their home pages, and ask them to add a link to yours.

Use traditional publicity methods. Write up a press release, and send it to media that report on the topic of your site. Don't forget newsletters and bulletins published by hobby groups. If it's appropriate, include your URL in advertisements, brochures, and other publicity materials.

Send information about your Web site to as many online directories and announcement services as possible. Start by pointing your Web browser to http://www.yahoo.com and clicking on the "Add URL" button. When the Add to Yahoo page appears, follow the instructions for sending them a description of your site.

Tell the world about your site.

After you submit your site description to Yahoo, return to the Yahoo home page and select Computers and Internet:Internet:World Wide Web:Announcement Services to see a list of other directories and "what's new" lists. Some of these sites want you to pay them for listings, but many more are free. Follow as many of these links as possible, and send each of them a description of your Web site.

WEB PAGES ON PRIVATE NETWORKS

> This is a free country, madam. We have a right to share your privacy in a public place.
>
> Sir Peter Ustinov
> *Romanoff and Juliet*, 1956

The Internet and the World Wide Web are not the only place you can use HTML documents. If your PC is connected to a LAN, you can use most of the features of HTML to circulate information within your work group or company. Many businesses are using HTML to allow employees to obtain copies of business forms, interactive policy manuals, technical manuals and specifications, and other internal documents.

There are two ways to do this:

1. Create a private TCP/IP network.
2. Use conventional LAN connections.

The TCP/IP approach is more flexible, but it's also a lot more expensive. If you don't need the other features and services that a TCP/IP network would give you, LAN distribution is a better option.

Private TCP/IP networks

If your LAN supports TCP/IP, you can place HTML documents on a Web server and let your users access them just as they would visit Web sites on the public Internet. You can even allow customers or off-site workers to dial into your TCP/IP network through modems, using SLIP or PPP connections. The only difference between a private TCP/IP network and a network connected to the Internet is the Internet backbone connection.

To set up a private TCP/IP network, you'll need a connectivity software package that includes both server and client programs for each of the services you want to provide to your users, along with administrative programs to handle things like domain name resolution. Among others, IBM, WRQ, FTP Software, NetManage, Frontier Technologies, Distinct, and TGV all offer connectivity packages. You'll also need to install and maintain your own Web server.

Hypertext through a LAN

The other approach, LAN connection, is a lot easier. Because it's possible to access files on other computers through a LAN, you can place HTML document files anywhere on the network and encourage other users to open these "local files" with a Web browser.

When you create HTML documents for use on a LAN, use the Local Document tab in the HyperLink <A> dialog box to create all of your hypertext links. Click on the Network button to add links to a network drive.

If you plan to distribute more than two or three groups of HTML documents, it's a good idea to designate one computer on the LAN as your document server. Create a separate directory on the server for each department within your organization and a subdirectory for each group of pages. Of course, you can include links in your documents to other text and data files that are located anywhere on the network.

USING HTML FOR DOCUMENT DISTRIBUTION

> There are no handles to a horse, but the 1910 model has a string to each side of its face for turning its head when there is anything you want it to see.
>
> Stephen Leacock
> *Literary Lapses*, "Reflections on Riding," 1910

There's one more thing you can do with HTML documents. Rather than storing your Web pages on a hard drive connected to a network, you can put hypertext documents on a floppy disk or a CD-ROM. The document must be self-contained, with no links or pointers to any other URL or drive letter, but if you use nothing but relative links, you can provide a tremendous amount of information to your readers very efficiently.

Keep your links in the same directory.

As you know, a hypertext link can point to a file in the same directory as the current document, or to any other location connected to the current document through a network. If you limit your links to the current directory, or subdirectories within the current directory, you can create a self-contained set of files. The Web browser program (which is, of course, really an HTML client that doesn't have to use the World Wide Web) is just as happy using relative links as jumping around the Internet—in fact, it will take less time to find a file on a local disk than to download it from another computer.

This is a slick method for creating and distributing interactive catalogs, technical manuals, and other complex information. Because you already know how to use Word and Internet Assistant, you don't have to learn a separate hypertext language. Your readers don't have to load a special program to read your files because they can use Word (with Internet Assistant) or any other Web browser, such as Mosaic or Netscape.

For example, you could create a list of products or parts, with hot links to individual product data sheets, installation procedures, and full-screen pictures of the item. In scholarly papers or journals distributed on CD-ROM, footnotes and cross-references can be direct links to other documents. A textbook or other "instructional media" (aren't buzzwords fun?) might include a set of questions for the reader, with links to the correct answers.

If you decide to try this, remember that Web browsers are not public domain programs. Before you can duplicate and distribute a browser, you must obtain specific permission from the copyright owner. If your readers have access to the Internet, it's probably easier to give them instructions for downloading a browser from online sources.

In this chapter, we've explained how to make your Web pages and other HTML documents available to other people. That's really the point of the whole exercise, isn't it? Unless somebody actually uses your Web pages, there's not much reason to create them.

The remaining chapters of this book describe some of the advanced HTML editing functions that Internet Assistant left out and provide information about the Windows 95 version of Internet Assistant.

10 What Internet Assistant Can't Do

If you want to get on in this world, make many promises but don't keep them.

Napoleon
Maxims, 1804–1815

Non-standard standards

As you explore other people's Web sites, you will probably notice that many of them have text formatted in ways that you haven't learned to do with Internet Assistant. There's a good reason for this: Internet Assistant doesn't include all of the latest and greatest formatting tags. Many of these new tags were defined by Netscape Communications, but they're not included in the official HTML specification. Some will probably be in the next version of the standard, but for the moment they're in a sort of limbo—several of the most popular Web browser programs recognize these formats, but others do not.

Remember the Cajun restaurant home page we visited in Chapter 3? The one that loses most of its interesting design features when you open it with Internet Assistant's Web browser? That's a page that includes Netscape extensions. Others are even worse jumbles with the "wrong" browser.

In this chapter, we'll talk about the tags and formats that Internet Assistant does not support and explain how to add them to your document. But first, let's see if we can make sense of the conflicting standards.

HTML 2, HTML 3, AND NETSCAPE EXTENSIONS: WHAT'S THE DIFFERENCE?

> Anything that is worth doing has been done frequently. Things hitherto undone should be given, I suspect, a wide berth.
>
> Sir Max Beerbohm
> *Mainly on the Air*, 1957

As I write this during the autumn of 1995, the only "official" HTML specification is HTML 1.0, which was adopted by the HTML Working Group of the World-Wide Web Consortium in 1993. But the way the World Wide Web is moving, a two-year-old standard is ancient history. The entire boom in Internet and World Wide Web access has taken place since then. HTML 2, which is currently in Final Review, is the one that's in common use today. The tags in Internet Assistant are consistent with HTML 2.

Netscape has altered the landscape.

When Netscape Communications introduced Netscape Navigator, they added a bunch of extra formatting tags to the standard set in HTML 2. These tags gave designers more tools to work with, but those tools only work with browsers that depart from the official standard. The unofficial tags are known as **Netscape extensions**. Many Web pages that use these extensions have "Optimized for Netscape" notices.

Net wars

As you might expect, the community of Web page designers is divided over this question. Since Netscape accounts for about 70 percent of all the hits on most Web sites, the people who use Netscape extensions figure that the bulk of their visitors will be able to see the fancy features they've included in their pages. The designers in the anti-Netscape extensions camp don't want to lose that other 30 percent of potential readers, who might otherwise be customers or converts to whatever cause their site is promoting.

To complicate matters even more, HTML 3, the next version of the official specification, will include many (but not all) of the Netscape extension tags and several more that the current release of Netscape does not recognize. So we'll soon have at least three different kinds of HTML documents:

1. **HTML 2**—The base-line set of formatting tags, recognized by all current browsers.

2. **Netscape Extensions**—The additional tags that add features that are not included in HTML 2.
3. **HTML 3**—The next-generation standard with many new features, including improved tables, figures, and forms; toolbars and static banners that don't scroll with the document; and support for languages that don't use the Roman alphabet (such as Russian, Chinese, and Japanese).

Do you want it fancy or do you want it universal?

Eventually, HTML 3 will probably either absorb or replace today's Netscape extensions, but for the moment, a Web page author faces a trade-off between pages that anybody can read and pages with complex design elements. If you limit yourself to the formatting tools in Internet Assistant, the decision has been made for you.

However, if you want to use Netscape extensions or other tags, you can use Word and Internet Assistant to create the basic structure of the page and then add the special tags by hand. In the next section, I'll explain how to add tags that are not on the Internet Assistant menus and toolbar. Keep in mind, however, that Internet Assistant is really not the right tool for the job.

If you can find one, you'll find it a lot easier to use an HTML editor program that includes all of the formatting tags you expect to use. You can find information about one promising contender, InContext Spider, at http://www.incontext.ca.

ADDING TAGS TO A WEB PAGE MANUALLY

> The test of a vocation is the love of the drudgery it involves.
>
> Logan Pearsall Smith
> *Afterthoughts*, 1931

If you decide to insert additional HTML tags to a document created with Internet Assistant, you won't see their effect until you open the document with a Web browser that recognizes those tags. In Internet Assistant's Web Browse view, text with an unknown tag will appear as if it had a Normal tag. As Figure 10.1 shows, Edit View displays <<Unknown HTML Tag>> after you save and reopen the file. To see the tag itself, double-click on the <<Unknown HTML Tag>> flag.

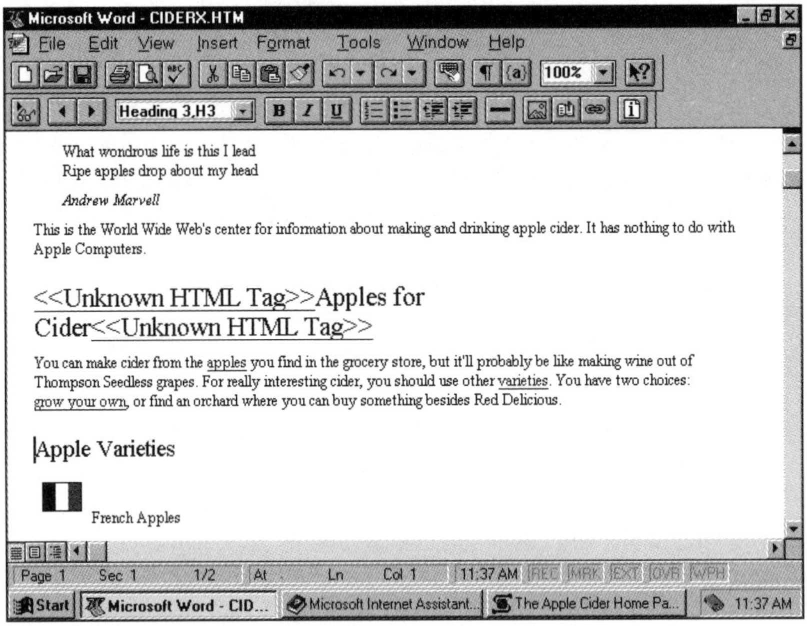

Figure 10.1 Special tags in Edit mode.

To insert special HTML tags into a document, follow these steps:

1. Place the cursor at the location where you want the tag.
2. Open the Insert menu and select the HTML Markup command. The dialog box in Figure 10.2 will appear.

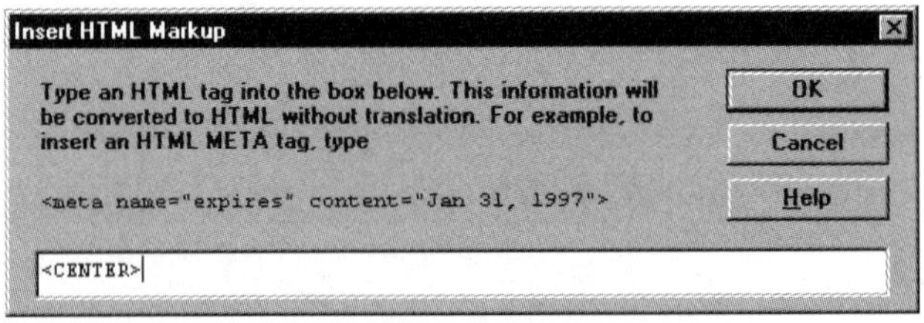

Figure 10.2 The Insert HTML Markup dialog box.

3. Type the text of the tag you want to insert, including the opening and closing angle brackets.
4. Click the OK button to close the dialog box.

Remember that most formatting tags require a second "end format" tag at the end of the text string to be formatted. For example, if you insert a <CENTER> tag, you must also insert a </CENTER> tag at the end of the text you want to center.

NETSCAPE EXTENSION TAGS

> All bad precedents began as justifiable measures.
>
> Julius Caesar
> quoted in *The Conspiracy of Cataline* by Sallust, c. 50 BC

In spite of the complications, you've chosen to use one or more of the unsupported tags. We'll explain the most useful Netscape extensions in this section, and some likely HTML 3 tags in the next. For a more detailed list of Netscape extensions, download the Extensions to HTML 2.0 documents from http://home.Netscape.com/assist/net_sites/html_extensions.html.

Tables

Tables: find another method

Chapter 6 described using PRE tags to create a table on a Web page. Netscape has added tags for much more complex tables.

Even more than most other features that other browsers ignore, information formatted into a table is really ugly and hard to read with the wrong browser because all of the information fields in the table will be jammed together. Worse than that, tables are confusing and complicated to build without a tool that shows you what you're doing. They're especially awful in Internet Assistant because you'll see a bunch of <<Unknown HTML Tag>> flags surrounding the text, headers, caption, rows, borders, and every other element of the table. For example, the table in Figure 10.3 is pretty simple—three cells wide by two high.

Now look at the mess, in Figure 10.4, that Internet Assistant makes of the same table.

Don't even try to make sense of constructing tables in Internet Assistant. It's hopeless. If you absolutely insist on adding a complex table to your Web page, find another tool that knows how to handle them.

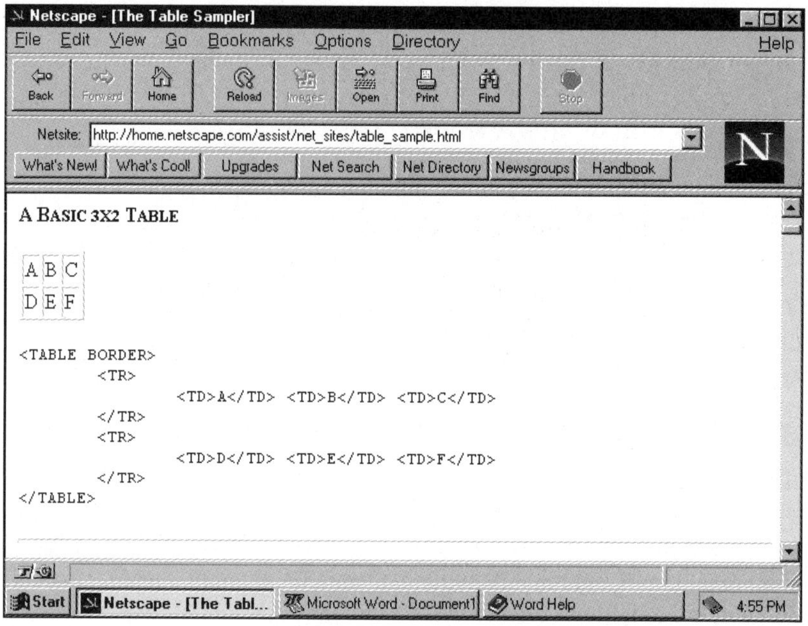

Figure 10.3 A simple table, as seen in Netscape.

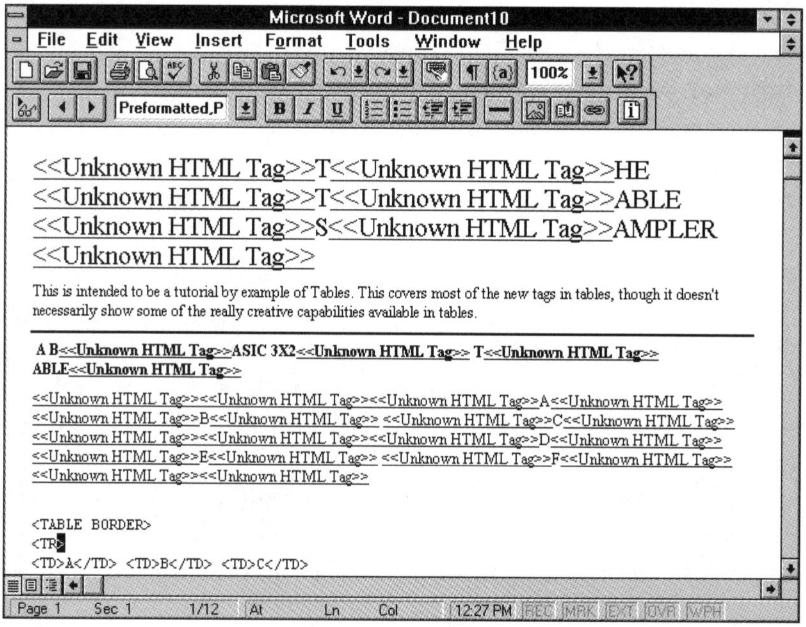

Figure 10.4 The same table, such as it is, in Internet Assistant's Edit mode.

There's still another problem with tables: the proposed specification keeps changing. So even if you hack your way through this month's swamp of table tags, they may not be the same in the next revision.

Background and Color Controls

Underneath it all

Not surprisingly, the "background" attributes change the background of an HTML document. The background can be a solid color or a pattern or graphic image. If you don't specify a background, the document will use the default solid color specified by the browser that displays it.

You can also specify the color of Normal text and the colors that a browser will use to display links. Once again, these specifications don't work on all Web browsers.

Color and background controls are one-time specifications; when you define them, they apply to the entire document. It's not possible to change colors within a page. These settings are probably not worth the trouble in Internet Assistant 1.0. They're a lot easier in Version 2, because Microsoft has added background and color controls. See Chapter 11 for more information about these new features.

The color and background attributes go inside the <BODY> tag that must appear just below the </HEADER> tag. The reason you can't have more than one background color on a document is that there's just one <BODY> tag. Since you can't see the <BODY> tag in View mode, you'll have to open and edit the file as text in Word rather than as an HTML document in Internet Assistant. This is a nuisance. But wait. It gets worse.

Solid Color Background

Solid backgrounds

You would think that specifying a solid color would be easy. Just <COLOR=RED> or something like that. But you have to specify the color in such an incredibly complicated format that you may want to simply forget the whole thing. The attribute for a solid background color is BGCOLOR, followed by the numeric red-green-blue (RGB) values of the color you want, converted to hexadecimal (base 16). You can find the decimal RGB numbers for a color by opening Display Properties from the Windows Control Panel, but you'll need a scientific calculator to convert those values to hexadecimal.

The format for the solid color background attribute is:

```
<BODY BGCOLOR="#rrggbb">
Document
</BODY>
```

Background Images

Pattern backgrounds

The alternative to a solid color background is an imported graphic image. Netscape and other browsers use this image as tiles that repeat to fill up the background of the page. Some designers go a little crazy with backgrounds, but you must choose them carefully to make sure they don't interfere with the foreground text. The wrong background can make a document difficult or even impossible to read.

Remember that the background image comes from a separate URL, which the browser must download before it can display your page. Don't use large, complex image files because they can take a long time to transfer.

The format for a tiled-image background is:

```
<BODY BACKGROUND="image.gif">   [Use the full URL of the image file
Document                         in place of image.gif]
</BODY>
```

Normal Text Color

Text colors

As I said, the color of the background can make the foreground text difficult to read. So you can change the text color by using this attribute:

```
<BODY TEXT="#rrggbb">
Document
</BODY>
```

Once again, you have to calculate the hexadecimal RGB value of the color you want before you can use this attribute.

Link Text Colors

The LINK, VLINK, and ALINK attributes control the color of link text, visited links, and active links, respectively. When you put all of these attributes together, the BODY attribute will look like this:

```
<BODY BGCOLOR="#000000" TEXT="F0F0F0" LINK="FFFF00"
 VLINK="#0F0F0F" ALINK="00FF00">
```

Figure 10.5 shows a Web page with a dark tiled background and white text.

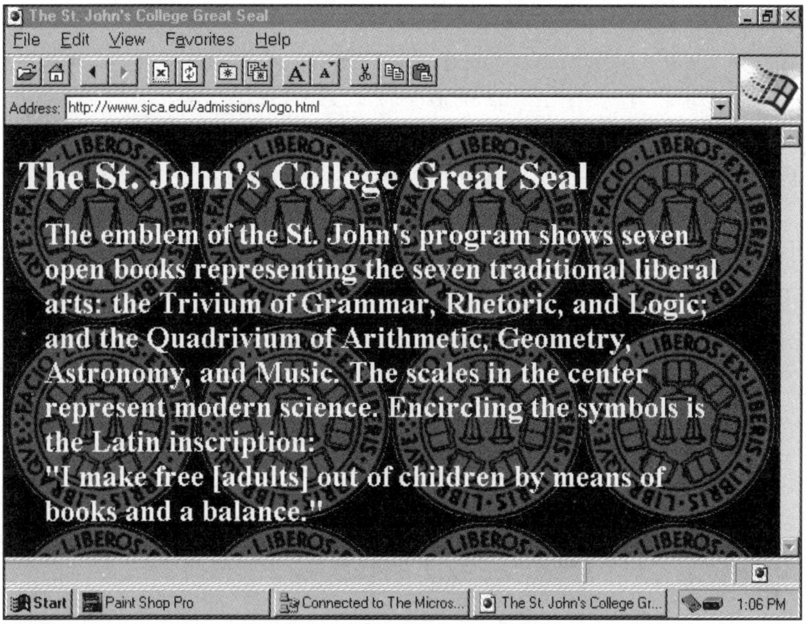

Figure 10.5 A tiled background and light color text.

Horizontal Rules

There's a Horizontal Line command in Internet Assistant, but it does not give you any options. All the lines are the same—what the specification calls a **shaded engraved line**. Netscape has come up with four new tags that specify the appearance of the line: **Rules rule.**

- **<HR SIZE=*number*>**—The SIZE attribute controls the thickness of the line, in pixels. The default thickness, which you get if you don't include a SIZE attribute, is two pixels.
- **<HR WIDTH=pixels | percent>**—The WIDTH attribute controls the width of the line, as either a number of pixels or a percentage of the page width.

- **<HR ALIGN=left | right | center>**—The ALIGN attribute is used with WIDTH to place a partial line at the left margin, the right margin, or the center of the screen.
- **<HR NOSHADE>**—NOSHADE instructs the browser to display a solid black line rather than the normal engraved line.

Bullet Shapes

Bite the bullet.

The List Bullet,UL command in Internet Assistant does not specify the shape of the bullets. You can add a TYPE to the <UL> tag to tell the browser what kind of bullet to use. You choices are <UL TYPE=DISC>, <UL TYPE=CIRCLE>, and <UL TYPE=SQUARE>.

Ordered Lists

When you use Internet Assistant's List Number,OL command, each item in the list gets a number. If you add a TYPE instruction to the tag, you can specify other numbering methods:

<OL TYPE=A>	Capital letters (A,B,C…)
<OL TYPE=a>	Small letters (a,b,c…)
<OL TYPE=I>	Large Roman numerals (I,II,III,IV…)
<OL TYPE=i>	Small Roman numerals (i,ii,iii,iv…)
<OL TYPE=1>	Arabic numbers (1,2,3…)

Font Sizes

Hard to read type in one easy lesson

Netscape allows you to change the relative size of individual letters or words within a block of text. The default font size is 3, within a range of 1 through 7. So you would use <FONT SIZE=1> for tiny type or <FONT SIZE=7> for huge type. Remember that many browsers won't do anything with these attributes, so you're better off using the six Heading tags instead.

A complete Font Size specification would look like this:

```
This sentence is normal size. <FONT SIZE=6> This sentence is
huge.</FONT> And this one is back to normal.
```

It would look like this on the screen:

This sentence is normal size. **This sentence is huge.** And this one is back to normal.

Centered Text

Centering

To center a headline or a block of text, use the <CENTER> tag at the beginning of the text and </CENTER> at the end.

Blinking Text

How to irritate your readers

I will probably regret telling you about <BLINK> if I ever visit your Web site and it blinks at me. If a browser recognizes it, the text between <BLINK> and </BLINK> flashes on and off like a blinking light. It's supposed to call attention to the flashing text, but it's really distracting when you're trying to read something else on the same page.

People who use <BLINK> are usually trying to say "Hey, look what I can do!" but the effect is more like those idiots who drive around in cars with the radio playing too loud (why don't those people ever play Scarlatti or the Modern Jazz Quartet?).

Image Alignment

ALIGN= commands

The new image alignment commands instruct the browser to wrap text around a picture. ALIGN=LEFT places the picture at the left margin, with text on the right; ALIGN=RIGHT puts the image on the right margin, with text on the left. The ALIGN= command should be located within the IMG tag that specifies the URL of the image, so you'll have to edit the document as text rather than using the Insert HTML Markup command.

Image Spacing

Space around images

Image spacing inserts some white space (or whatever color your background is) between an image and the surrounding text. VSPACE=*pixels* places space above and below the image. HSPACE=*pixels* inserts space on the left or right. Once again, this attribute goes within the IMG tag.

Image Borders

Borders To place a line around picture or other graphic image, use the command BORDER=*pixels* within the IMG tag. Don't set BORDER=0 on an image link, or you'll eliminate the colored border that identifies it as a link.

HTML 3 FEATURES

> What we call "progress" is the exchange of one nuisance for another nuisance.
>
> Havelock Ellis

HTML 3 is still in development, so there will almost certainly be many more changes before it becomes official. But some browsers are beginning to include some HTML 3 attributes, so you might want to consider using them in your documents.

In particular, there are two useful new font style tags:

- <BIG>...</BIG>—Text within the BIG tags is (surprise!) a bigger font than the standard for the current paragraph.
- <SMALL>...</SMALL>—As you'd expect, SMALL text is smaller than normal.

ALTERNATIVES TO INTERNET ASSISTANT

> If people have to choose between freedom and sandwiches, they will take sandwiches.
>
> Lord John Boyd-Orr, 1955

Other Web page editors Internet Assistant is not the only HTML editor out there. Developing Web pages is this year's growth industry, so there are lots of people making tools for the developers. Some, like Internet Assistant, are freebies, whereas others have prices ranging from about $100 for InContext Spider to $7500 (!) for InterNotes for Lotus Notes. These programs are not necessarily any better than Internet Assistant, but they do offer different approaches to the process.

You can find a reasonably complete list of HTML editors (with links to the home pages for each one) at http://union.ncsa.uiuc.edu/HyperNews/get/www/html/editors.html. Here are some other online sources for information about specific HTML editors:

InContext Spider	http://www.incontext.ca
HoTMetal	http://www.softquad.com
Quarterdeck WebAuthor	http://www.qdeck.com
Nice Tech WebWizzard	http://infolane.com
HTML Assistant	http://fox/ntsn.ca/~harawitz/index.html
HTML Writer	http://lal.cs.byu.edu/people/nosack
HTMLed	ftp://tenb.mta.ca/pub/HTMLed/
Live Markup	http://www.mediatec.com/mediatech/
WebEdit	http://ww.thegroup.net/webedit.htm

11 Coming Attractions: Internet Assistant for Word 7

If the package doesn't say "New" these days, it had better say "Seven Cents Off."

Spencer Klaw
Fortune magazine, 1963

While I was writing this book, the folks at Microsoft were busy creating a new version of Internet Assistant to go along with Windows 95 and Word 7 (also known as Word 95). The new release is also compatible with Word 6.0 for Windows NT. If you're still using Word 6, you can skip this chapter, but you might want to skim it to see if any of the new features are enough to convince you to go out and spend the money on upgrades for Windows and Word.

Microsoft made the first "beta test" version of Internet Assistant 2.0 available to the public at the same time that they released Windows 95 and Word 7 because they didn't want people to use Internet Assistant as an excuse for not buying the Windows and Word upgrades. Like most beta software, the version I used to prepare this chapter is not complete. Microsoft has promised to add even more new features in the "final release," but if I had waited to see them, you wouldn't be reading this book today.

Amazing... an upgrade that's an improvement

To their credit, the Internet Assistant team has replaced most of the worst features of the earlier version, while keeping the good parts. They've also added support for several of the most important HTML extensions that were missing from Version 1. Painful as it is to actually say something nice about Microsoft, Version 2 of Internet Assistant has all the signs of becoming a solid, well-thought-out HTML editor. The new Internet Assistant Web browser is a huge improvement over the earlier version, but it's still not as good as Netscape, Mosaic, or Microsoft's own Internet Explorer.

It's still free. Like its predecessor, Internet Assistant 2.0 is available at no cost. The URL for the Internet Assistant home page on the World Wide Web is http://www.microsoft.com/msoffice/freestuff/msword-/download/ia/default.htm. You should also be able to find it on CompuServe, America Online, Microsoft Network, GEnie, or the Microsoft Download Service (206-936-6735). The filename of the beta version is wordia2b.exe. When the final release comes out, it will probably be wordia2z.exe.

Version 2.0 of Internet Assistant includes these new features and functions:

- Installation that is consistent with Windows 95 conventions
- Improved View HTML Source
- A browser that imports Web pages more quickly
- Centering for text and images
- Background images and color
- Text and link color control

By the time the final release version of Version 2.0 appears, Microsoft has promised to add support for still more new HTML extensions. They've also announced that the product will have "improved Windows 95 look and feel," but they haven't explained exactly what that means.

INSTALLING INTERNET ASSISTANT 2.0

> We should distrust any enterprise that requires new clothes.
>
> Henry David Thoreau
> *Walden*, 1854

In order to install and use Internet Assistant 2.0, you should already have the following software on your computer:

- Windows 95 or Windows NT
- Word 7 for Windows 95 or Word 6.0 for Windows NT

Urdu and Icelandic users are out of luck.

This version of Internet Assistant is compatible with the English, French, German, and Italian versions of Word. If your computer works with Windows 95 or Windows NT, you should already have enough computing power and memory to handle Internet Assistant.

Internet Assistant's Web browser requires a connection to the Internet through a 32-bit Winsock interface. The Winsock stack supplied with Windows 95 works well with Internet Assistant, but you will have a problem if you're using an older 16-bit Internet access product such as Trumpet Winsock, NetManage Chameleon, or Internet in a Box. (Winsock interfaces are explained in Chapter 3.) If you're not sure what kind of Winsock you've got, talk to your LAN administrator or your Internet service provider.

Assuming you've already installed Windows 95 and Word 7 (or Windows NT and Word 6), here's what you should do to install Internet Assistant:

1. If you're upgrading from Internet Assistant 1.0, make a backup copy of the Favorite.doc file in your Old Word Documents\Internet directory.
2. If you haven't already obtained a copy of Internet Assistant 2.0, download it now.
3. Open the folder that contains the wordia2*x*.exe file, and double-click on the file icon.

The executable Internet Assistant file will expand the necessary files and start the Setup routine. As questions appear on your screen, answer them. When Setup is complete, it will display the information window in Figure 11.1.

New location

One of the differences between Version 1.0 and Version 2.0 is the location of the Internet Assistant files. In Version 1.0, they're in a subdirectory called Internet within the Word directory. In Version 2.0, most of the files are in a separate folder under Program Files. Since you won't ever open Internet Assistant without opening Word first, this doesn't really make any difference to the way you use the program, but it does follow the rules for organizing program files in Windows 95.

If you ever need to remove Internet Assistant, open Add/Remove Programs from the Windows Control Panel, and select Microsoft Internet Assistant from the list of programs in the Install/Uninstall dialog box.

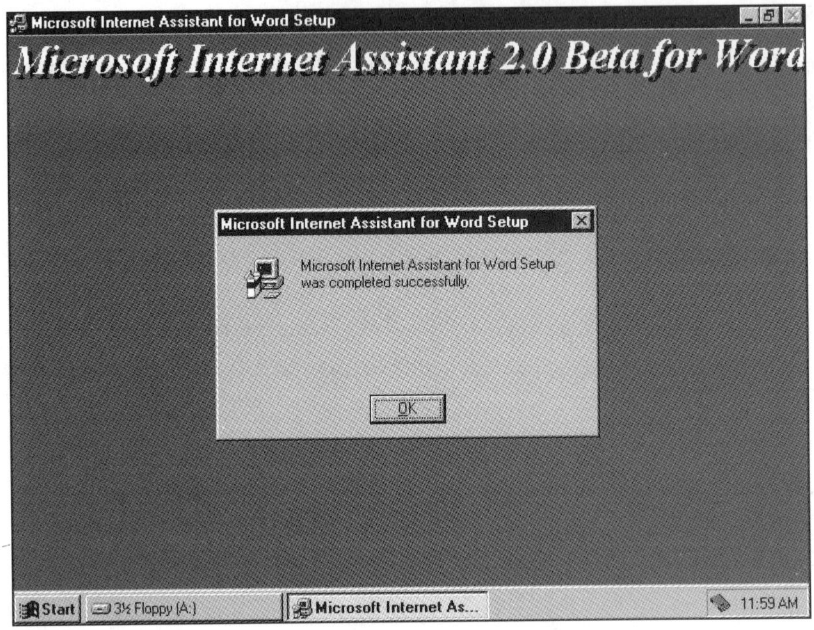

Figure 11.1 The Setup Complete information window.

Nice, easy-to-remember filenames

Within Word, Internet Assistant loads the same way as it did in Version 1, but the Global Template has a new name: WIAHTM32.WLL. Trips off the tongue easily, doesn't it? Sure it does. To turn Internet Assistant on or off, use the Templates command in the File menu and add or remove the checkmark next to the filename, as shown in Figure 11.2.

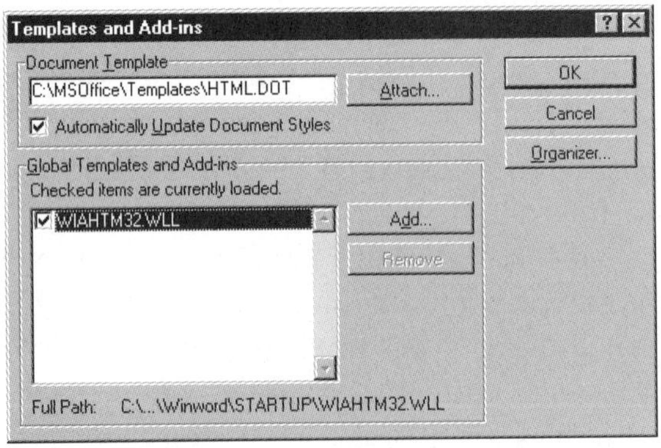

Figure 11.2 The Templates and Add-ins dialog box.

THE IMPROVED WEB BROWSE MODE

> Some men are born mediocre, some men achieve mediocrity, and some men have mediocrity thrust upon them.
>
> Joseph Heller
> *Catch-22*

Improved browser

Web Browse mode looks almost the same as it did in Version 1.0. The Title button is gone from the formatting toolbar, and there are a couple of new commands, but everything else that I described in Chapter 3 is still there. However, the internal plumbing is new, and it works a lot better than it did before. The new browser imports Web pages from the Internet substantially faster than the one it replaces. But that's not to suggest that Word and Internet Assistant are serious competition for the top-of-the-heap browsers like Mosaic and Netscape. Version 1 was a mediocre Web browser; Version 2 is better, but it's still a mediocre Web browser.

Navigating the World Wide Web

Figure 11.3 shows Web Browse mode. As you can see, it looks very much as it did in Version 1.0.

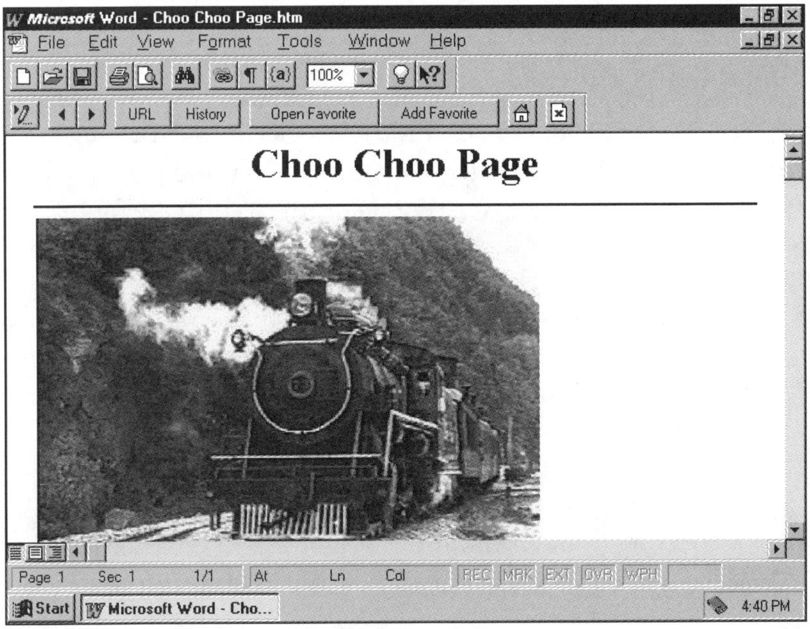

Figure 11.3 Word in Web Browse mode.

There's one new feature: Web Browse view now recognizes the <CENTER> tag, so you won't see nearly as much image text scrunched over to the left margin. As Figure 11.4 shows, tables are still a problem.

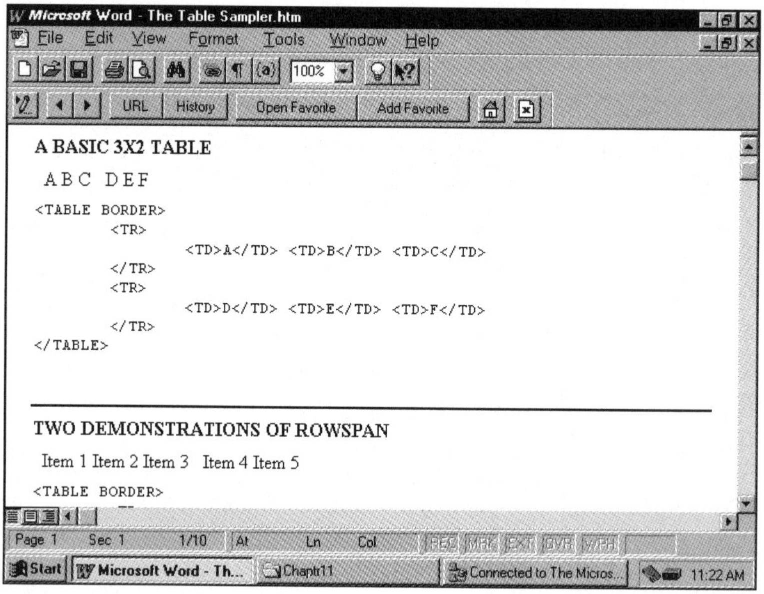

Figure 11.4 Internet Assistant still doesn't recognize tables.

Finding a Better Browser

Get your own copy of Netscape.

Internet Assistant no longer uses InternetWorks as its browsing engine, so there's no longer a separate Web browser hidden on your hard drive. That's no great loss, but it means that you can forget about everything in Chapter 4 of this book. InternetWorks is still available, in a version called GNNWorks that's far superior to the one that was in Internet Assistant. It's now part of America Online's Global Network Navigator package. In the unlikely event that you've become attached to that particular screen layout, take a look at http://gnn.com for information about obtaining GNN software.

If you don't already have a stand-alone Web browser, you should find one right away. Among the browsers that you can buy at your local software store, I like Netscape Navigator and Quarterdeck's version of Mosaic; of the ones you can download through the Internet,

Netscape (http://home.netscape.com) and NCSA Mosaic (http://www.ncsa.uiuc.edu/SDG/Software/Mosaic/NCSAMosaic-Home.html) are my current favorites.

NEW HTML EXTENSIONS

> The race is not always to the swift, nor the battle to the strong, but that's the way to bet.
>
> Damon Runyon

Netscape extensions

As yet another proof that Netscape is the 800-pound gorilla of the World Wide Web, Microsoft has included support for several of Netscape's extensions to the HTML 2.0 specification in the new version of Internet Assistant. Even though these extensions are not part of the official standard, the great majority of browsers will recognize them. All of these new commands are in Edit View. You can use them when you create a new document, or to change the appearance of an existing page.

Centering

Center Align

The Align Left and Align Center commands control the horizontal placement of any element in your HTML document. The <CENTER>…</CENTER> tags are separate from the Style tags, so you can apply any style to centered text.

To center a paragraph, place your cursor anywhere within the paragraph and select the Center Align command from the Format menu, or click the Center button in the formatting toolbar. To move the text to the left margin, use the Align Left command or button.

You can also use the Align Left and Align Center commands on images within your Web pages. To center a picture, click on it and choose the Center Align command.

Background Color and Images

No more RGB codes

You can now specify a solid color or tiled image background for your Web page in Internet Assistant, but you won't be able to see the result until you open the document with another browser. To add either a

BACKGROUND or BGCOLOR attribute to your page, open the Format menu and select the Background and Links command to display the dialog box in Figure 11.5.

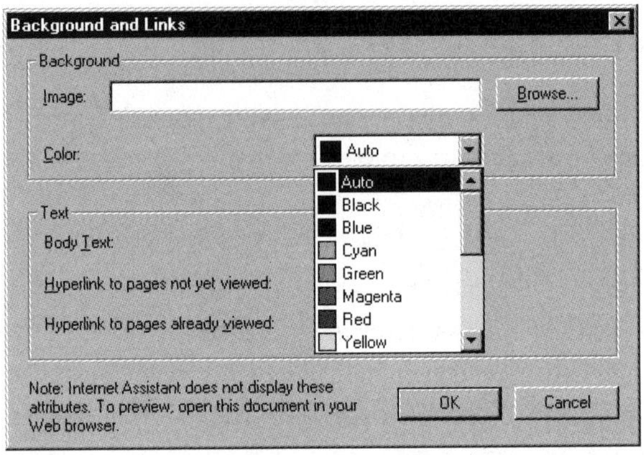

Figure 11.5 The Background and Links dialog box.

For a tiled image background, type the relative path of the image file in the Image field, or use the Browse button to select a file from a directory.

The Color command replaces the colossal nuisance of specifying a background color as a hexidecimal RGB value with a simple drop-down menu. Choose a color from the menu, or select Auto to allow each browser that downloads the page to use its default color.

Text and Link Colors

Text colors When you change the background color, you must also remember to specify text colors that provide enough contrast. The Text block in the Background and Links dialog box adds TEXT, LINK, and VLINK attributes to the <BODY> tag. Like the Background command, these text commands automatically insert the ugly hexadecimal RGB color values from a menu of colors.

VIEWING HTML TAGS AND SOURCE CODE

> The three questions of greatest concern are:
>
> 1. Is it attractive?
> 2. Is it amusing?
> 3. Does it know its place?
>
> Fran Lebowitz
> *Metropolitan Life*, 1978

Another important new feature of Version 2.0 is the HTML Source command in the View menu. When you select this command, Word opens a new window that contains the current document as straight text, including all of the HTML formatting tags and attributes, as shown in Figure 11.6. This is a great improvement over the old method, which required saving and closing the document, reopening it as a text file, saving it again, and reopening once again as HTML.

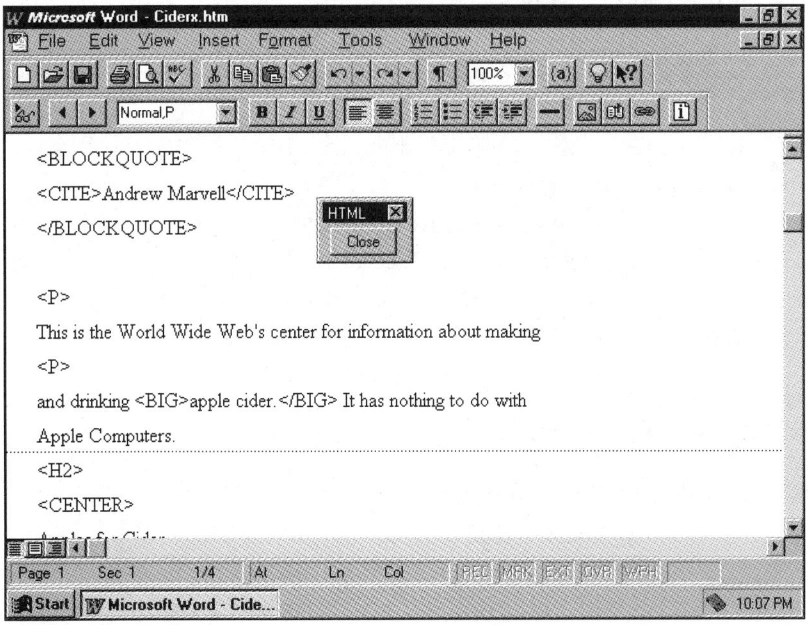

Figure 11.6 HTML Source View.

When you open HTML Source View, there's a toolbox with a Close button in the middle of the screen. It's in the most inconvenient place possible, right on top of the text. The first thing you should do with this screen is to drag the toolbox to the top of the screen, which will add the Close button to your toolbar.

Source View is an editor.

You can use all of Word's text editing functions in HTML Source View. As a result, it's a convenient way to add Netscape extensions and other tags that Internet Assistant does not support, and to make minor changes to existing tags. For example, you could add the <BIG>...</BIG> style element to a text string by simply typing the tags at the beginning and end of the text that you want to enlarge.

When you work in Source View, remember that you're editing a text file without any kind of formatting. Don't try to apply styles from the formatting toolbar; you'll lose them when you return to Edit View.

It's entirely possible to create Web pages and other HTML documents without ever using HTML Source View. But when a client or boss insists that you include some obscure new attribute that they've seen on somebody else's Web page, it offers a quick and easy way to jump in and adjust the document's code.

To return to Edit View, click on the Close button. Word will save the document and reopen it as formatted HTML.

Now... real tags!

In Edit View, Internet Assistant now displays the actual tags that it does not recognize (Figure 11.7), rather than the obnoxious <<Unknown HTML Tag>> marker that appeared in Version 1.0. When you switch to Web Browse View, the program still ignores mystery tags.

OTHER NEW FEATURES

Progress was all right; it just went on too long.

James Thurber

Watch for updates.

As I said earlier in this chapter, Microsoft is still working on Internet Assistant 2.0, so it will probably have some additional features by the time you read this. At the top of my wish list, I'm hoping the final version includes support for tables, Horizontal Rule attributes, and more detailed help screens.

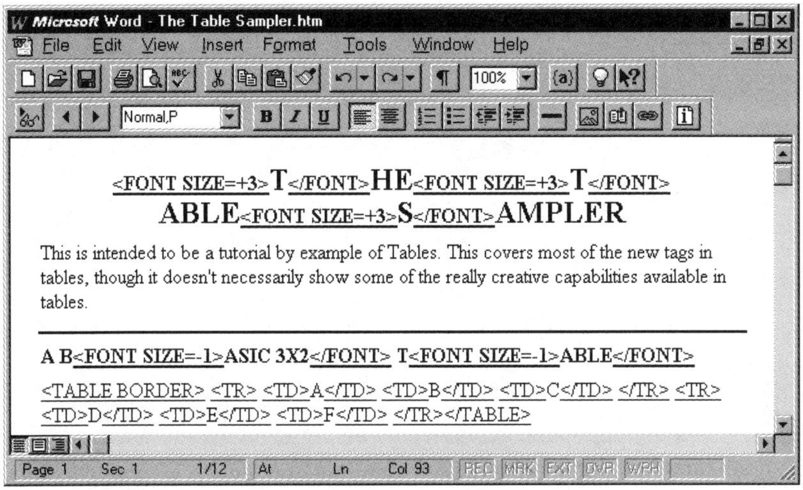

Figure 11.7 A Web page with unrecognized tags.

It's a good idea to check the Microsoft Web site every so often to see if a newer release has appeared. Since the program is a freebie, there's really no excuse not to have the latest version.

Appendix

HTML Tags and Internet Assistant Commands

This appendix contains a list of HTML tags with the equivalent Internet Assistant command for each one.

Style commands are located in the Style menu in the Edit View formatting toolbar.

Tag	Function	Command or Style
<A>	Anchor	
<A HREF=...>	Hyperlink	Insert>Hyperlink
<A Name=...>	Bookmark	Edit>Bookmark 
<ADDRESS>	Address	Address
<B>	Bold type	
<BLOCKQUOTE>	Quoted text	Blockquote
<BODY>	Body text	None; added automatically
 	Line break	Shift-Enter
<CENTER>*	Center text or image	Format>Center Align 
<CITE>	Citation	Cite
<CODE>	Code text	Code
<DD>	Definition	None; applied automatically
<DFN>	Definition	Definition,DFN
<DIR>	Directory	Directory,DIR
<DL>	Definition List	Definition List,DL
<DL COMPACT>	Compact Definition List	Definition Compact,DLC
<DT>	Definition Term	None; applied automatically
<EM>	Emphasis	Emphasis,EM
<FORM>	Form Field	Insert>Form Field

*Internet Assistant Version 2 only

Tag	Function	Command or Style
<H1> through <H6>	Heading 1 through 6	Heading 1 through 6
<HEAD>	HTML Document Heading	None; applied automatically
<HR>	Horizontal Rule	Horizontal Rule,HR
<HTML>	HTML Document	None; applied automatically
<I>	Italic type	
<IMG>	Insert an Image	Insert>Picture
<KBD>	Keyboard Font	Keyboard,KBD
<LI>	List Item	None; applied automatically
<MENU>	Menu List	Menu
<META>	"Meta" Non-printing text	File>HTML Document Info
<OL>	Ordered List	List Number,OL
<P>	Body Text Paragraph	Normal,P
<PRE>	Preformatted Text	Preformatted
<PRE WIDTH=>	Preformatted Text with specified width	Preformatted - Wide
<SAMP>	Sample Text	Sample,SAMP
<STRIKE>	Strikethrough Type	Strikethrough,STRIKE
<STRONG>	Strong Type	Strong,STRONG
<TITLE>	Document Title	
<TT>	Typewriter Font	Typewriter,TT
<U>	Underline Type	
<UL>	Unordered (bulleted) list	List Bullet,UL
<VAR>	Variable Text	Variable,VAR

Index

G

H

N

O

P